FREDERICK COUNTY VIRGINIA

MILITIA RECORDS 1755-1761

I0109254

Barbara Vines Little

HERITAGE BOOKS
2007

HERITAGE BOOKS

AN IMPRINT OF HERITAGE BOOKS, INC.

Books, CDs, and more—Worldwide

For our listing of thousands of titles see our website
at
www.HeritageBooks.com

Published 2007 by
HERITAGE BOOKS, INC.
Publishing Division
65 East Main Street
Westminster, Maryland 21157-5026

International Standard Book Number: 978-1-58549-558-0

An Act
For the Better Regulating and Training of the Militia

In August 1755 the General Assembly of Virginia passed an act for the better regulating and training of the militia. This act replaced an older act that had proved ineffectual. The following is a short summary of the major points of the act. The full text can be found in William Waller Hening's *The Statutes at Large, Volume VI* (Richmond, 1819), pages 530-542.

All county lieutenants, colonels, lieutenant colonels and other inferior officers, bearing any commission in the militia of the colony, were to be inhabitants of and resident in the county where they were commissioned.

The lieutenant, or in his absence, the chief officer of the militia in every county was to list all the male persons, above the age of eighteen years and under the age of sixty years (imported servants excepted).

The following people were not expected to muster: members of the council: speaker of the house of Burgesses; receiver general; auditor; secretary; attorney general; clerk of the council; clerk of the secretary's office; ministers of the Church of England; the president, masters or professors, and students of William and Mary College; the mayor, recorder, and aldermen of the city of Williamsburg and the borough of Norfolk; and the keeper of the public goal; any person being an overseer over four servants or slaves and actually residing on the plantation where they work and receiving a share of the crop or wages; any miller having the charge and keeping of any mill; and founders, keepers or other persons employed in or about any copper, iron or lead mine.

All people enlisted except the people commonly called Quakers, free Mulattoes, negroes and Indians and placed or ranked in the horse or foot were to be armed and accoutered as follows: horsemen with a serviceable horse, a good saddle, with a breast-plate, crupper and curb bridle, carbine and bucket, holsters, a case of pistols, cutting sword, double cartouche box and six charges of powder; and footmen with a firelock well-fixed, a bayonet fitted to the same, a cutting sword, a double cartouche box and three charges of powder. In addition, one pound of powder and four pounds of ball were to be kept at the place of abode and brought into the field when required. The county was to send to England for arms for those too poor to provide their own. (These were to be paid for out of the next county levy.)

Every captain was to call a private muster every three months or oftener. Two general musters (March and September) were to be called by the chief commanding officer in the county.   Horsemen were to be fined 10 shillings for non-appearance and 5 shillings for appearing without proper arms and accoutrements. Footmen were fined 7 shilling 6 pence for non-appearance and 3 shillings for appearance without proper arms and accoutrements.

Every captain was to make a list of all the persons upon his muster-roll who though summoned did not appear at any of the said musters properly armed and accoutred. This list was to be returned to the next court martial. Failure to do so resulted in a fine of ten pounds.

Court martials were to be conducted at the courthouse the day following the general muster in September. The court had the power to exempt such as they judged incapable of service and to remit fines levied by the preceding court martial for just excuses. The court was required to keep a register of the proceedings.

The following pages were abstracted from a microfilm copy of the Frederick County, Virginia, register.

Frederick County Early Troop Record 1755-1761[1]

[page 1] At a Court Martial held for the County of Frederick on Tuesday the 2d day of September 1755 present

The Right Honble **Thomas Lord Fairfax** county Lieutenant
George William Fairfax Colonel
Thomas Bryan Martin Lieutenant Colonel
Meridith Helm Major

Richard Morgin	**Jacob Funk Junr**	
Jeremiah Smith	**Samuel Odell**	
Jacob Funk	**William Bethel**	
Issaac Parkin	**Edward Rodgers**	Captains
John Hardin	**John Linsey**	
Cornilias Ruddell	**William Vance**	
Lewis Stephen	**John Dinton**	

Robert Rutherford appointed Clerk of the Court Martial
William Vance Captain of Foot Returned his List of Delinquents

Ordered that **John House** of the foot company Commanded by **Capt William Vance** be fined Five shillings or fifty lbs of Tob° for absenting himself from one private Muster within twelve Months Last Past[2]

Samuel Gann of the foot company Commanded by **Capt William Vance** ... Five shillings or fifty lbs Tobo ... one private ....

Philip Harker of the foot company Commanded by **Capt William Vance** ... Five shillings or fifty lbs Tob° ... one private ....

John Duckworth of the foot company Commanded by **Capt William Vance** ... Five shillings or fifty lbs Tob° ... one private ....

Simon Carson of the foot company Commanded by **Capt William Vance** ... Five shillings or fifty lbs Tob° ... one private ....

[page 1-A] On the petition of **John Morgan** a foot soldier of the Company commanded by **Captain William Vance** ordered that he be Discharged being unfit for duty

On the Motion of **James Calvil** a foot soldier in the Company Commanded by **Capt William Vance** Ordered that he be Discharged from Doing Duty

---

[1] Taken from Virginia State Archives Microfilm Reel 9 (Frederick Co.) following Deed Book 18.

[2] This is the form used for all fines. In the following abstracts only the types of musters missed and the amount of the fine is given.

John Funk Captain of Foot returned his List of Delinquents

Gotlip Gabbert in the foot Company Commanded by **Capt John Funk** ... Five shillings or fifty lbs Tob° ... one general ....

George Seller in the foot Company Commanded by **Capt John Funk** ... Five shillings or fifty lbs Tob° ... one general ....

Stephen Nowland in the foot Company Commanded by **Capt John Funk** ... Five shillings or fifty lbs Tob° ... one general ....

Jacob Bowman in the foot Company Commanded by **Capt John Funk** ... Five shillings or fifty lbs Tob° ... one general ....

Henry Fravel in the foot Company Commanded by **Capt John Funk** ... Five shillings or fifty lbs Tob° ... one general ....

George Rust in the foot Company Commanded by **Capt John Funk** ... fifteen shillings or 150 lb Tob° ... three privates ...

Rynard Bodden in the foot Company Commanded by **Capt John Funk** ... Five shillings or fifty lbs Tob° ... one general ....

[page 2] **Nehimiah Odell** in the foot Company Commanded by **Capt John Funk** ...Five shillings or fifty lb Tob° ... one general ....

Robert Gray in the foot Company Commanded by **Capt John Funk** ... Ten shillings or one hundred lb tob° ... two private ...

Tehobald Fight in the foot Company Commanded by **Capt John Funk** ... ten shillings or 100 lb tob°...one private & one general ....

John Hanks in the foot Company Commanded by **Capt John Funk** ... Five shillings or fifty lbs Tob° ... one general ....

John Marty in the foot Company Commanded by **Capt John Funk** ... Ten shillings or 100 lb tob° ...private & one general ....

John Miller tanner in the foot Company Commanded by **Capt John Funk** ... Five shillings or fifty lbs Tob° ... one general ....

Jeremiah Smith Captain of Foot returned his List of Delinquents

Thomas Pugh in the foot company of **Capt Jeremiah Smith** ... 100 weight of tobacco or ten shillings ... two private ....

James Howart in the foot company of **Capt Jeremiah Smith** ... fifteen shillings or 150 pounds of tobacco ... two private & one general ....

[page 2-A] **George Rubel** in the foot company of **Capt Jeremiah Smith** ...Ten shillings or 100 lb tob° ... private & one general ....

Daniel Pritchard in the foot company of **Capt Jeremiah Smith** ... five shillings or fifty lb tobo ... one private muster ....

James McCoy in the foot company of **Capt Jeremiah Smith** ... Five shillings or fifty lb tob° ... one private muster ....

William Harry in the foot company of **Capt Jeremiah Smith** ... Five shillings or fifty lb tob° ...one private muster ....

On the motion of **Christopher Smallsoffer** a foot soldier of the Company Commanded by **John Funk** ordered that he be discharged from Doing Duty

Azariah Pugh of Company Commanded by **Capt Jeremiah Smith** ... ten shillings or 100 pounds of tobacco ... two private ....

Richard Morgin Captain of foot Returned his List of Delinquents

John Heywood of the foot company commanded by **Capt Richard Morgin** ... five shillings or fifty lb tob° ... one general ....

Moses Heywood of the foot company commanded by **Capt Richard Morgin** ... Five shillings or fifty lb tob° ... one general ....

Anthony Turner Senr of the foot company commanded by **Capt Richard Morgin** ... Five shillings or fifty lb tob° ... one general ....

[page 3] **Anthony Turner Junr** of the foot company commanded by **Capt Richard Morgin** ... Five shillings or fifty lb tob°...one general....

Remimbrance Williams of the foot company commanded by **Capt Richard Morgin** ... Five shillings or fifty lb tob°... one general ....

Regnal Green of the foot company commanded by **Capt Richard Morgin** ... Five shillings or fifty lb tob° ... one general ....

Thomas Hart Junr of the foot company commanded by **Capt Richard Morgin** ... Five shillings or fifty lb tob° ... one general ....

James Loyd of the foot company commanded by **Capt Richard Morgin** ... Five shillings or fifty lb tob° ... one general ....

Leonard Saverrel of the foot company commanded by **Capt Richard Morgin** ... Five shillings or fifty lb tob° ... one general ....

John Linsey Captain of a Troop returned his List of Delinquents

William Jolliff Junr of the Company Commanded by **Capt John Linsey** ... Seven shillings & six pence or 75 lb tob°...one private....

John Marpool ... Seven shillings & six pence or 75 lb tob° ... one

Jeremiah Archer of the Company Commanded by **Capt John Linsey** ... seven shillings & six pence or 75 lb tob° ... one private ....

Daniel Marshall of the Company Commanded by **Capt John Linsey** ... seven shillings & six pence or 75 lb tob° ... one private ....

Thomas Green of the Company Commanded by **Capt John Linsey** ... seven shillings & six pence or 75 lb tob° ... one private ....

George Tollis of the Company Commanded by **Capt John Linsey** ... seven shillings & six pence or 75 lb tob° ... one private ....

John Ridgway of the Company Commanded by **Capt John Linsey** ... seven shillings & six pence or 75 lb tob° ... one private ....

Morriss Reece Senr of the Company Commanded by **Capt John Linsey** ... seven shillings & six pence or 75 lb tob° ... one private ....

Morriss Reece Junr of the Company Commanded by **Capt John Linsey** ... seven shillings & six pence or 75 lb tob° ... one private ....

Richard Reves of the Company Commanded by **Capt John Linsey** ... seven shillings & six pence or 75 lb tob° ... one private ....

Lewis Stephen Captain of foot Returned his List of Delinquents [page 4] **Joseph Colvil** of the Company Commanded by **Cap' Lewis Stephen** ... five shillings or fifty lb tob° ... one private ....

John Reed of the Company Commanded by **Cap' Lewis Stephen** ... ten shillings or 100 lb tob° ... two private ....

James Wilson of the Company Commanded by **Cap' Lewis Stephen** ... ten shillings or 100 lb tob° ... one private & one general ....

William Snell of the Company Commanded by **Cap' Lewis Stephen** ... fifteen shillings or 150 lb tob° ... two private & one general ....

George Wright Sen' of the Company Commanded by **Cap' Lewis Stephen** ... fifteen shillings or 150 lb tob° ... two private & one general ....

David Wright of the Company Commanded by **Cap' Lewis Stephen** ... fifteen shillings or 150 lb tob° ... two private & one general ....

George Wright Jun' of the Company Commanded by **Cap' Lewis Stephen** ... ten shillings or 100 lb tob° ... one private & one general ....

Jacob Christman of the Company Commanded by **Cap' Lewis Stephen** ... ten shillings or 100 lb tob° ... two private ....

[page 4-A] **John Mires** of the Company Commanded by **Cap' Lewis Stephen** ... five shillings or fifty lb tob° ... one general ....

On the motion of **John Snap Sen'** a foot soldier in the Company Commanded by **Cap' Lewis Stephen** ordered that he be Discharged from doing Duty

Isaac Parkin Captain of foot returned his List of Delinquents

Thomas Babb of the Company Commanded by **Cap' Isaac Parkin** ... ten shillings or 100 lb tob° ... one private & one general ....

James Jolliff of the Company Commanded by **Cap' Isaac Parkin** ... five shillings or fifty lb tob° ... one general ....

William Hicks of the Company Commanded by **Cap' Isaac Parkin** ... ten shillings or 100 lb tob° ... two private ....

John Baylery of the Company Commanded by **Cap' Isaac Parkin** ... ten shillings or 100 lb tob° ... two private ....

Siman Owerson of the Company Commanded by **Cap' Isaac Parkin** ... ten shillings or 100 lb tob° ... one private & one general ....

David Shanes of the Company Commanded by **Cap' Isaac Parkin** ... five shillings or fifty lb tob° ... one private ....

Robert Hodson of the Company Commanded by **Cap' Isaac Parkin** ... fifteen shillings or 150 lb tob° ... two private & one general ....

[page 5] **John Hails** of the Company Commanded by **Cap' Isaac Parkin** ... five shillings or fifty lb tob° ... one private ....

Michael Caity of the Company Commanded by **Cap' Isaac Parkin** ... five shillings or fifty lb tob° ... one private ....

George Thomas of the Company Commanded by **Cap' Isaac Parkin** ... ten shillings or 100 lb tob° ... two private ....

Willam Sample of the Company Commanded by **Capt Isaac Parkin** ... ten shillings or 100 lb tob° ... one private & one general ....

John Job of the Company Commanded by **Capt Isaac Parkin** ... ten shillings or 100 lb tob° ... one private & one general ....

Robt Stuart of the Company Commanded by **Capt Isaac Parkin** ... five shillings or fifty lb tob° ... one general ....

Thomas Eldridge of the Company Commanded by **Capt Isaac Parkin** ... five shillings or fifty lb tob° ... one general ....

Thomas Cambell of the Company Commanded by **Capt Isaac Parkin** ... five shillings or fifty lb tob° ... one general ....

John McGudgion of the Company Commanded by **Capt Isaac Parkin** ... five shillings or fifty lb tob° ... one general ....

Alexander Bradey of the Company Commanded by **Capt Isaac Parkin** ... five shillings or fifty lb tob° ... one general ....

[page 5-A] **Isaac Buston** of the Company Commanded by **Capt Isaac Parkin** ... five shillings or fifty lb tob° ... one general ....

Thomas Babb Junr of the Company Commanded by **Capt Isaac Parkin** ... five shillings or fifty lb tob° ... one general ....

George Holingsworth of the Company Commanded by **Capt Isaac Parkin** ... five shillings or fifty lb tob° ... one general ....

On the Motion of **Joseph Hubbs** a foot soldier in the company commanded by **Capt Isaac Parken** Ordered that he be Discharged from doing Duty

Edward Rogers Captain of foot returned his List of Delinquents

Ordered that **John Wood** a Serjiant in the foot Company Commanded by **Capt Edward Rogers** ... be fined ... two private ....

Isaac Stokes of the Company Commanded by **Capt Edward Rogers** ... five shillings or fifty lb tob° ... one private ....

Joseph Combs of the Company Commanded by **Capt Edward Rogers** ... five shillings or fifty lb tob° ... one private ....

Samuel Timons of the Company Commanded by **Capt Edward Rogers** ... five shillings or fifty lb tob° ... one private ....

[page 6] **James Bryn** of the Company Commanded by **Capt Edward Rogers** ... five shillings or fifty lb tob° ... one private ....

Edward Jinnins of the Company Commanded by **Capt Edward Rogers** ... five shillings or fifty lb tob° ... one private ....

Thomas Howell of the Company Commanded by **Capt Edward Rogers** ... fifteen shillings or 150 lb tob° ... one private & one general ... & for not appearing at an other private muster armed & accoutered as the law directs ....

Joseph George of the Company Commanded by **Capt Edward Rogers** ... five shillings or fifty lb tob° ... one private ....

George Arnold of the Company Commanded by **Capt Edward Rogers** ... five shillings or fifty lb tob° ... one private ....

Richard Johnson of the Company Commanded by **Capt Edward Rogers** ... five shillings or fifty lb tob° ... one private ....

Humphrey Hopkins of the Company Commanded by **Capt Edward Rogers** ... ten shillings or 100 lb tob° ... one private ... & for not appearing at an other private muster properly armed & accoutered as the law directs ....

Joseph Borden of the Company Commanded by **Capt Edward Rogers** ... fifteen shillings or 150 lb tob° ... three private ....

Thomas Posegate of the Company Commanded by **Capt Edward Rogers** ... five shillings or fifty lb tob° ... one private ....

[page 6-A] Ordered that **John Waters** of the foot company commanded by **Capt Edward Rogers** be fined

Richard Holmes of the Company Commanded by **Capt Edward Rogers** ... ten shillings or 100 lb tob° ... one private muster & another armed & accoutered as the law directs ....

Joseph McCarty of the Company Commanded by **Capt Edward Rogers** ... five shillings or fifty lb tob° ... one general ....

Benjamin Kelly of the Company Commanded by **Capt Edward Rogers** ... five shillings or fifty lb tob° ... one private ....

George Henry of the Company Commanded by **Capt Edward Rogers** ... five shillings or fifty lb tob° ... one private muster armed & accoutered as the law directs ....

Thomas Bennet of the Company Commanded by **Capt Edward Rogers** ... five shillings or fifty lb tob° ... one private muster armed & accoutered as the law directs ....

On the motion of **Darbey Murphey** a foot soldier in the Company Commanded by **Capt Edward Rodgers** Ordered that he be Discharged from doing Duty

John Harden Captain of foot returned his List of Delinquents

William Daves of the Company Commanded by **Capt John Harden** ... five shillings or fifty lb tob° ... one private ....

[page 7] **Benjamin Makall** of the Company Commanded by **Capt John Harden** ... ten shillings or 100 lb tob° ... two private ....

Humphrey Keys of the Company Commanded by **Capt John Harden** ... ten shillings or 100 lb tob° ... two private ....

Abraham Hains of the Company Commanded by **Capt John Harden** ... ten shillings or 100 lb tob° ... two private ....

William Rankins of the Company Commanded by **Capt John Harden** ... ten shillings or 100 lb tob° ... two private ....

Benjamin Pearson of the Company Commanded by **Capt John Harden** ... twenty shillings or 200 lb Tob° ... four private ....

Samuel Pearson of the Company Commanded by **Capt John Harden** ... fifteen shillings or 150 lb tob° ... three private ....

Samuel Brittain of the Company Commanded by Capt John Harden ... twenty shillings or 200 lb Tob° ... four private ....

John Humphrys of the Company Commanded by Capt John Harden ... ten shillings or 100 lb tob° ... two private ....

[page 7-A] **William Price** of the Company Commanded by Capt John Harden ... five shillings or fifty lb tob° ... one private ....

Benjamin Satterfield of the Company Commanded by Capt John Harden ... five shillings or fifty lb tob° ... one private ....

John Vastal of the Company Commanded by Capt John Harden ... fifteen shillings or 150 lb tob° ... Three private ....

Edmund Lindsey Junr of the Company Commanded by Capt John Harden ... five shillings or fifty lb tob° ... one private ....

James Dunbar of the Company Commanded by Capt John Harden ... twenty shillings or 200 lb Tob° ... four private ....

Duggell McQuin of the Company Commanded by Capt John Harden ... twenty shillings or 200 lb Tob° ... four private ....

Charles Worrill of the Company Commanded by Capt John Harden ... fifteen shillings or 150 lb tob° ... two private & one general ....

John Hultz [Thiltz] of the Company Commanded by Capt John Harden ... five shillings or fifty lb tob° ... one private ....

James Cator of the Company Commanded by Capt John Harden ... five shillings or fifty lb tob° ... one private ....

[page 8] **Peter Poulson** of the Company Commanded by Capt John Harden ... five shillings or fifty lb tob° ... one private ....

William Cocks Captain of a Troop returned his List of Delinquents

George Hampton of the Company Commanded by Capt William Cocks ... seven shillings six pence or 75 lb tob° ... one general ....

Nathaniel Daugherty of the Company Commanded by Capt William Cocks ... seven shillings six pence or 75 lb tob° ... one general ....

Joseph Hampton ... seven shillings & six pence or 75 lb tob° ... one general ....

William Roberts of the Company Commanded by Capt William Cocks ... seven shillings & six pence or 75 lb tob° ... one general ....

John Scot of the Company Commanded by Capt William Cocks ... seven shillings & six pence or 75 lb tob° ... one general ....

Absalam Hammon of the Company Commanded by Capt William Cocks ... seven shillings & six pence or 75 lb tob° ... one general ....

John Davis of the Company Commanded by Capt William Cocks ... seven shillings & six pence or 75 lb tob° ... one general ....

[page 8-A] **Pattrick McDaniel** of the Company Commanded by Capt William Cocks ... seven shillings & six pence or 75 lb tob° ... one general ....

John Mounts of the Company Commanded by Capt William Cocks ... seven shillings & six pence or 75 lb tob° ... one general ....

Thomas Davis of the Company Commanded by **Capt William Cocks** ... seven shillings & six pence or 75 lb tob° ... one general ....

John Bell of the Company Commanded by **Capt William Cocks** ... seven shillings & six pence or 75 lb tob° ... one general ....

James King of the Company Commanded by **Capt** William Cocks ... seven shillings & six pence or 75 lb tob° ... one general ....

John Loyd of the Company Commanded by **Capt William Cocks** ... seven shillings & six pence or 75 lb tob° ... one general ....

On the motion of **Hugh Fox** a Soldier of the troop Commanded by **Capt Wm Cocks** Ordered that he be discharged from Doing Duty

Cornelius Ruddell Captain of Foot returned His List of Delinquents

George Brock of the Company Commanded by **Capt Cornelius Ruddle** ... five shillings or fifty lb tob° ... one general ....

[page 9] **Thomas Gill** of the Company Commanded by **Capt Cornelius Ruddle** ... five shillings or fifty lb tob° ... one general ....

Burger Minor of the Company Commanded by **Capt Cornelius Ruddle** ... five shillings or fifty lb tob° ... one general ....

James Brittain of the Company Commanded by **Capt Cornelius Ruddle** ... five shillings or fifty lb tob° ... one general ....

Benjamin Brackseller of the Company Commanded by **Capt Cornelius Ruddle** ... five shillings or fifty lb tob° ... one general ....

Jacob Moore of the Company Commanded by **Capt Cornelius Ruddle** ... five shillings or fifty lb tob° ... one general ....

Jacob Funk Captain of foot returned his list of Delinquents

John Little of the Company Commanded by **Capt Jacob Funk** ... five shillings or fifty lb tob° ... one general ....

Henry Cloud of the Company Commanded by **Capt Jacob Funk** ... five shillings or fifty lb tob° ... one general ....

Edward Grymes of the Company Commanded by **Capt Jacob Funk** ... five shillings or fifty lb tob° ... one general ....

[page 9-A] **John Branson** of the Company Commanded by **Capt Jacob Funk** ... ten shillings or 100 lb tob° ... two general ....

William Branson of the Company Commanded by **Capt Jacob Funk** ... ten shillings or 100 lb tob° ... one general & one private ....

Jacob Hannon of the Company Commanded by **Capt Jacob Funk** ... five shillings or fifty lb tob° ... one general ....

Peter Edwards of the Company Commanded by **Capt Jacob Funk** ... five shillings or fifty lb tob° ... one general ....

Moses Harrol of the Company Commanded by **Capt Jacob Funk** ... five shillings or fifty lb tob° ... one general ....

Richard Harrol of the Company Commanded by **Capt Jacob Funk** ... five shillings or fifty lb tob° ... one general ....

William Priest of the Company Commanded by **Capt Jacob Funk** ... ten shillings or 100 lb tob° ... one general & one private ....

Adam Seller of the Company Commanded by **Capt Jacob Funk** ... five shillings or fifty lb tob° ... one general ....

Phillip Self of the Company Commanded by **Capt Jacob Funk** ... five shillings or fifty lb tob° ... one general ....

[page 10] **Joseph Ballinger** of the Company Commanded by **Capt Jacob Funk** ... five shillings or fifty lb tob° ... one general ....

John Denton Captain of Foot returned his List of Delinquents

Frederick Wolfat of the Company Commanded by **Capt John Denton** ... five shillings or fifty lb tob° ... one private muster properly armed & accoutered as the law directs ....

James McKenny of the Company Commanded by **Capt John Denton** ... ten shillings or 100 lb tob° ... one private muster properly armed & accoutered as the law directs & one general ....

Mark Voltz of the Company Commanded by **Capt John Denton** ... five shillings or fifty lb tob° ... one private muster properly armed & accoutered as the law directs ....

John Mire of the Company Commanded by **Capt John Denton** ... five shillings or fifty lb tob° ... one private muster armed & accoutered as the law directs ....

John Miller of the Company Commanded by **Capt John Denton** ... five shillings or fifty lb tob° ... one private muster properly armed & accoutered as the law directs ....

John Closime of the Company Commanded by **Capt John Denton** ... five shillings or fifty lb tob° ... one private muster armed & accoutered as the law directs ....

Peter Funk of the Company Commanded by **Capt John Denton** ... five shillings or fifty lb tob° ... one private muster armed & accoutered as the law directs ....

[page 10-A] **David Rodinhaver** of the Company Commanded by **Capt John Denton** ... five shillings or fifty lb tob° ... one private muster properly armed & accoutered as the law directs ....

George Little of the Company Commanded by **Capt John Denton** ... five shillings or fifty lb tob° ... one private muster armed & accoutered as the law directs ....

Augustine Coffman of the Company Commanded by **Capt John Denton** ... five shillings or fifty lb tob° ... one private muster armed & accoutered as the law directs ....

George Coffield of the Company Commanded by **Capt John Denton** ... five shillings or fifty lb tob° ... one private muster armed & accoutered as the law directs ....

Vallentine Coffield of the Company Commanded by **Capt John Denton** ... five shillings or fifty lb tob° ... one private muster armed & accoutered as the law directs ....

Henry Black of the Company Commanded by **Capt John Denton** ... five shillings or fifty lb tob° ... one private muster armed & accoutered as the law directs ....

Martin Roller of the Company Commanded by **Capt John Denton** ... five shillings or fifty lb tob° ... one private muster armed & accoutered as the law directs ....

John Bayly of the company Commanded by **Capt John Denton** ... ten shillings or 100 lb tob° ... one private muster armed & accoutered as the law directs & one general ....

Richard Nicholas of the company Commanded by **Capt John Denton** ... five shillings or fifty lb tob° ... one private muster armed & accoutered as the law directs ....

Henry Peters of the company Commanded by **Capt John Denton** ... five shillings or fifty lb tob° ... one private muster armed & accoutered as the law directs ....

[page 11] **Ulrick Bealor** of the company Commanded by **Capt John Denton** ... five shillings or fifty lb tob° ... one private muster armed & accoutered as the law directs ....

John Painter of Stoney Creek of the company Commanded by **Capt John Denton** ... ten shillings or 100 lb tob° ... one private muster armed & accoutered as the law directs & one general ....

George Anman of the company Commanded by **Capt John Denton** ... five shillings or fifty lb tob° ... one private muster armed & accoutered as the law directs ....

Frederick Fisher of the company Commanded by **Capt John Denton** ... five shillings or fifty lb tob° ... one private muster armed & accoutered as the law directs ....

John Dotson of the company Commanded by **Capt John Denton** ... five shillings or fifty lb tob° ... one private muster armed & accoutered as the law directs ....

Stephen Shoeman of the company Commanded by **Capt John Denton** ... five shillings or fifty lb tob° ... one private muster armed & accoutered as the law directs ....

Jacob Nodle of the company Commanded by **Capt John Denton** ... five shillings or fifty lb tob° ... one private muster armed & accoutered as the law directs ....

Henry Burge of the company Commanded by **Capt John Denton** ... five shillings or fifty lb tob° ... one private muster armed & accoutered as the law directs ....

[page 11-A] **Anthony Stultz** of the company Commanded by **Capt John Denton** ... ten shillings or 100 lb tob° ... one private muster armed & accoutered as the law directs ... one general ....

Nicholas Countz of the company Commanded by **Capt John Denton** ... ten shillings or 100 lb tob° ... one private muster armed & accoutered as the law directs ... one general ....

Henry Countz of the company Commanded by **Capt John Denton** ... ten shillings or 100 lb tob° ... one private muster armed & accoutered as the law directs ... & one general ....

Abraham Miller of the company Commanded by **Capt John Denton** ... ten shillings or 100 lb tob° ... one private & one general ....

William Rodgers of the company Commanded by **Capt John Denton** ... ten shillings or 100 lb tob° ... one private one general ....

Jacob Miller of the company Commanded by **Capt John Denton** ... five shillings or fifty lb tob° ... one general ....

Ulrick Thinah [Kinah] of the company Commanded by **Capt John Denton** ... ten shillings or 100 lb tob° ... one private & one general ....

Adam Fox of the company Commanded by **Capt John Denton** ... five shillings or fifty lb tob° ... one private ....

George Hoffman of the company Commanded by **Capt John Denton** ... ten shillings or 100 lb tob° ... one private & one general ....

[page 12] **Peter Bowman** of the company Commanded by **Capt John Denton** ... ten shillings or 100 lb Tob° ... one private & one general ....

Patrick McCaib of the company Commanded by **Capt John Denton** ... ten shillings or 100 lb Tob° ... one private & one general ....

Morgan Jones of the company Commanded by **Capt John Denton** ... ten shillings or 100 lb Tob° ... one private & one general ....

Andrew Maden of the company Commanded by **Capt John Denton** ... ten shillings or 100 lb Tob° ... one private & one general ....

Frederick Dillingar of the company Commanded by **Capt John Denton** ... ten shillings or 100 lb Tob° ... one private & one general ....

Charles Taylor of the company Commanded by **Capt John Denton** ... ten shillings or 100 lb Tob° ... one private & one general ....

Mark Ilor [ISor] of the company Commanded by **Capt John Denton** ... five shillings or fifty lb tob° ... one private ....

Samuel Nizely of the company Commanded by **Capt John Denton** ... ten shillings or 100 lb Tob° ... one private & one general ....

Phillip Goodbread of the company Commanded by **Capt John Denton** ... five shillings or fifty lb tob° ... one general ....

John Allison ... five shillings or fifty lb tob° ... one general ....

[page 12-A] **Samuel Odell** Captain of Foot returned his List of Delinquents

Joseph Abel Junʳ of the company Commanded by **Capt Samuel Odell** ... ten shillings or 100 lb Tob° ... one private & one general ....

Obadiah Hammons of the company Commanded by **Capt Samuel Odell** ... ten shillings or 100 lb Tob° ... one private & one general ....

Maxsamillion Bush of the company Commanded by **Capt Samuel Odell** ... ten shillings or 100 lb Tob° ... one private & one general ....

Robert Hammet of the company Commanded by **Capt Samuel Odell** ... five shillings or fifty lb tob° ... one general ....

William Jackson of the company Commanded by **Capt Samuel Odell** ... ten shillings or 100 lb Tob° ... one private & one general ....

Robert Edwards of the company Commanded by **Capt Samuel Odell** ... ten shillings or 100 lb Tob° ... one private & one general ....

Daniel Curtis of the company Commanded by **Capt Samuel Odell** ... ten shillings or 100 lb Tob° ... one private & one general ....

James Wallis of the company Commanded by **Capt Samuel Odell** ... ten shillings or 100 lb Tob° ... one private & one general ....

John Tollifer of the company Commanded by **Capt Samuel Odell** ... five shillings or fifty lb tob° ... one general ....

[page 13] **Isaac Wood** of the company Commanded by **Capt Samuel Odell** ... ten shillings or 100 lb Tob° ... one private & one general ....

William Wood of the company Commanded by **Capt Samuel Odell** ... ten shillings or 100 lb Tob° ... one private & one general ....

Joseph Cave of the company Commanded by **Capt Samuel Odell** ... ten shillings or 100 lb Tob° ... one private & one general ....

Daniel Stover of the company Commanded by **Capt Samuel Odell** ... five shillings or fifty lb tob° ... one private ....

Zachariah McCay of the company Commanded by **Capt Samuel Odell** ... fifteen shillings or 150 lb tob° ... two private & one general ....

Moses McCay of the company Commanded by **Capt Samuel Odell** ... fifteen shillings or 150 lb tob° ... two private & one general ....

On the motion of **Ralph Hughes** a foot Soldier in the Company Commanded by **Capt Samuel ODell** Ordered that He be Discharged from doing Duty

William Bethel Captain of foot returned his List of Delinquents

John Crume of the company Commanded by **Capt William Bethel** ... five shillings or fifty lb tob° ... one private ....

[page 13-A] **Edward Price** of the company Commanded by **Capt William Bethel** ... five shillings or fifty lb tob° ... one private ....

Jacob Lommonah of the company Commanded by **Capt William Bethel** ... ten shillings or 100 lb tob° ... two private ....

John Limeburger of the company Commanded by **Capt William Bethel** ... five shillings or fifty lb tob° ... one private ....

John Taylor of the company Commanded by **Capt William Bethel** ... five shillings or fifty lb tob° ... one private ....

Michael Comer of the company Commanded by **Capt William Bethel** ... ten shillings or 100 lb tob° ... two private ....

Michael Porough of the company Commanded by **Capt William Bethel** ... five shillings or fifty lb tob° ... one general ....

David Cotzman of the company Commanded by **Capt William Bethel** ... ten shillings or 100 lb tob° ... two private ....

Samuel Beam of the company Commanded by **Capt William Bethel** ... ten shillings or 100 lb tob° ... two private ....

Conrood Rich of the company Commanded by **Capt William Bethel** ... ten shillings or 100 lb tob° ... two private ....

[page 14] **Joseph Cambel** of the company Commanded by **Capt William Bethel** ... ten shillings or 100 lb tob° ... two private ....

Christian Harris of the company Commanded by **Capt William Bethel** ... ten shillings or 100 lb tob° ... two private ....

Henry Hustand of the company Commanded by **Capt William Bethel** ... ten shillings or 100 lb tob° ... two private ....

John Tann of the company Commanded by **Capt William Bethel** ... ten shillings or 100 lb tob° ... two private ....

Bostion Frederick of the company Commanded by **Capt William Bethel** ... ten shillings or 100 lb tob° ... two private ....

John Wood of the company Commanded by **Capt William Bethel** ... ten shillings or 100 lb tob° ... two private ....

Casper Brainer of the company Commanded by **Capt William Bethel** ... ten shillings or 100 lb tob° ... two private ....

Phillip Grubb of the company Commanded by **Capt William Bethel** ... ten shillings or 100 lb tob° ... two private ....

Benjamin Grisby of the company Commanded by **Capt William Bethel** ... five shillings or fifty lb tob° ... one private ....

[page 14-A] **Adam Voltz** of the company Commanded by **Capt William Bethel** ... ten shillings or 100 lb tob° ... two private ....

Christian Maggard of the company Commanded by **Capt William Bethel** ... ten shillings or 100 lb tob° ... two private ....

John Halterman of the company Commanded by **Capt William Bethel** ... ten shillings or 100 lb tob° ... two private ....

Phillip Baker of the company Commanded by **Capt William Bethel** ... ten shillings or 100 lb tob° ... two private ....

David Maggard of the company Commanded by **Capt William Bethel** ... ten shillings or 100 lb tob° ... two private ....

John Countz of the company Commanded by **Capt William Bethel** ... ten shillings or 100 lb tob° ... two private ....

Joseph Summers of the company Commanded by **Capt William Bethel** ... five shillings or fifty lb tob° ... one private ....

Philip Kiplinger of the company Commanded by **Capt William Bethel** ... ten shillings or 100 lb tob° ... two private ....

John Henry Pippin of the company Commanded by **Capt William Bethel** ... ten shillings or 100 lb tob° ... two private ....

[page 15] **Michael Mire** of the company Commanded by **Capt William Bethel** ... ten shillings or 100 lb tob° ... two private ....

Jacob Pontz of the company Commanded by **Capt William Bethel** ... ten shillings or 100 lb tob° ... two private ....

Peter Painter of the company Commanded by **Capt William Bethel** ... ten shillings or 100 lb tob° ... two private ....

John Low of the company Commanded by **Capt William Bethel** ... ten shillings or 100 lb tob° ... two private ....

Henry Pressor of the company Commanded by **Capt William Bethel** ... ten shillings or 100 lb tob° ... two private ....

Lewis Stonis of the company Commanded by **Capt William Bethel** ... ten shillings or 100 lb tob° ... two private ....

Jacob Strickler of the company Commanded by **Capt William Bethel** ... ten shillings or 100 lb tob° ... two private ....

Joseph Strickler of the company Commanded by **Capt William Bethel** ... ten shillings or 100 lb tob° ... two private ....

[page 15-A] **John Berry** of the company Commanded by **Capt William Bethel** ... ten shillings or 100 lb tob° ... two private ....

Daniel Kiplinger of the company Commanded by **Capt William Bethel** ... ten shillings or 100 lb tob° ... two private ....

Jacob Shaver of the company Commanded by **Capt William Bethel** ... ten shillings or 100 lb tob° ... two private ....

Charles Thompson of the company Commanded by **Capt William Bethel** ... ten shillings or 100 lb tob° ... two private ....

John Smith of the company Commanded by **Capt William Bethel** ... five shillings or fifty lb tob° ... one private ....

Archart Burner of the company Commanded by **Capt William Bethel** ... five shillings or fifty lb tob° ... one private ....

John Gotlip of the company Commanded by **Capt William Bethel** ... ten shillings or 100 lb tob° ... two private ....

Frederick Shober of the company Commanded by **Capt William Bethel** ... ten shillings or 100 lb tob° ... two private ....

[page 16] **Charles Hyzer** of the company Commanded by **Capt William Bethel** ... five shillings or fifty lb tob° ... one private ....

Then the Court Martial Adjourned until tomorrow Morning 8 oClock

                                                                          Fairfax

At a Court Martial held for Frederick County on Wednesday the 3^{d} day of September 1755

Present

The Right Honble The **Lord Fairfax** County Lieutenant
George William Fairfax Colonel
Thomas Bryan Martin Lieutenant colonel
John Hardin
William Vance
William Bethel
Cornelious Ruddell   Captains
John Funk jun^{r}
Samuel Odell
Thomas Swaringin

On the motion of **Richard Morley** a foot Soldier in the Company Comanded by **Capt Cornelius Ruddell** Ordered that he be Discharged from doing Duty

On the Motion of **Jacob Gimblet** a foot Soldier in the Company Commanded by **Capt Cornelius Ruddell** Ordered that he be Discharged from doing Duty

Captain Isaac Parkin is appointed Treasurer of the Court Martial

[page 16-A] Ordered that the Clerk Deliver the Sev^{l} Orders of the Court to the Sheriff in Order to collect according to Law & pay the same to the Treasurer & that the said Treasurer account for the same at the next Court Martail

Ordered that the Treasurer pay to the Clerk of the Court Martail the sum of 5£ out of the s^{d} fines as his Sallary

Ordered that the clerk provide a proper Record Book & that the Treasurer pay the said Clerk for the same out of the said fines.

At a Councel of War held for Regulating the Militia of Frederick County in order to take such steps as Shall be Thought Most Expediant on the Present Critical Conjuncture the 14th Day of April 1756

Present

The Right Honble The **Lord Fairfax** County Lieutenant
John Hite Major
John Lindsey
Isaac Parkin
Richard Morgin
Samuel Odell   Captains
Edward Rodgers
Jeremiah Smith
Thomas Caton
Paul Long

Proposals having been Sent to the several Captains of the Militia Signed by the Comanding officer of the said Malitia & Dated the 7th Day of April 1756 to set what Vollenturs they Could Encourage to go
[page 17] In Search of the Indian Enimy who are dayly ravaging our Fronteir & Commiting their accustomed Cruelties on the Inhabitants & the afforesaid Captains being Met together & finding the Number of Men insufficient to go out against the Enemy its Considered that the Men be Discharged being Only fifteen

Fairfax

At a Court Martial held for Frederick County on Fryday the 27th of October 1758

Present

The Right Honble The **Lord Fairfax** County Lieut^t
Thomas Bryan Martin Esqr Colonel
John Hite gentleman Lieu^t Colonel
William Vance Gentleman Major
John Funk
Isaac Perkins
John Hardin
Robert Pearis   Captains
Thomas Speak
Thomas Swearingin Junr
Henry Spears
Marquis Calmes

... Ordered that **Robert Rutherford** be appointed Clark of the Court Martial ....

[page 17-A]   [handwriting changes]
Capt Marquis Calemus Returned his muster role
John Painter Senr of the company Commanded by **Capt Marquis Calmemus** ... forty shillings ... three Private & one general ....
Edward Rodgers Senr... forty shillings of the company Commanded by **Capt Marquis Calmemus** ... three Private & one general ....
William Berry of the company Commanded by **Capt Marquis Calmemus** ... forty shillings ... three Private & one general ....
George Jamison of the company Commanded by **Capt Marquis Calmemus** ... forty shillings ... three Private & one general ....
Robert Painter of the company Commanded by **Capt Marquis Calmemus** ... forty shillings ... three Private & one general ....
Samuel Humber of the company Commanded by **Capt Marquis Calmemus** ... forty shillings ... three Private & one general ....
[page 18] **Robert Hains** of the company Commanded by **Capt Marquis Calmemus** ... forty shillings ... three Private & one general ....
George Rought of the company Commanded by **Capt Marquis Calmemus** ... forty shillings ... three Private & one general ....
Dennis Bon of the company Commanded by **Capt Marquis Calmemus** ... twenty shillings of the company Commanded by **Capt Marquis Calmemus** ... two private ....
David Lindsey of the company Commanded by **Capt Marquis Calmemus** ... thirty shilllings ... two private & one general ....
Nathaniel Curry of the company Commanded by **Capt Marquis Calmemus** ... twenty shillings ... two private ....
Jeremiah Wood of the company Commanded by **Capt Marquis Calmemus** ... ten shillings ... one private ....
Henry Hampton of the company Commanded by **Capt Marquis Calmemus** ... ten shillings ... one private ....
Joseph Combs of the company Commanded by **Capt Marquis Calmemus** ... ten shillings ... one private ....
Peter Rout of the company Commanded by **Capt Marquis Calmemus** ... ten shillings of the company Commanded by **Capt Marquis Calmemus** ... one private ....
Robert Goodlet of the company Commanded by **Capt Marquis Calmemus** ... twenty shillings ... one private & one general ....
Thomas Collins of the company Commanded by **Capt Marquis Calmemus** ... ten shillings ... one private ....
William Snell of the company Commanded by **Capt Marquis Calmemus** ... ten shillings ... one private ....
Joseph Borden of the company Commanded by **Capt Marquis Calmemus** ... ten shillings ... one private ....

Charles Baker of the company Commanded by **Capt Marquis Calmemus** ... ten shillings ... one private ....

[page 19] **Francis Howell** of the company Commanded by **Capt Marquis Calmemus** ... ten shillings ... one private ....

Moses Arnold of the company Commanded by **Capt Marquis Calmemus** ... ten shillings ... one private ....

Thomas George of the company Commanded by **Capt Marquis Calmemus** ... ten shillings ... one private ....

William Wood of the company Commanded by **Capt Marquis Calmemus** ... ten shillings ... one private ....

James King of the company Commanded by **Capt Marquis Calmemus** ... twenty shillings ... one private & one general ....

George Seabourn of the company Commanded by **Capt Marquis Calmemus** ... twenty shillings ... one private & one general ....

Abraham Miller of the company Commanded by **Capt Marquis Calmemus** ... twenty shillings ... one private & one general ....

[page 19-A] **Isaac Stokes** of the company Commanded by **Capt Marquis Calmemus** ... ten shillings ... one general ....

Hasle Hardwick of the company Commanded by **Capt Marquis Calmemus** ... ten shillings ... one general ....

John Temmons of the company Commanded by **Capt Marquis Calmemus** ... ten shillings ... one general ....

Benjamin Wood of the company Commanded by **Capt Marquis Calmemus** ... ten shillings ... one general ....

Joseph Wood of the company Commanded by **Capt Marquis Calmemus** ... ten shillings ... one general ....

Cap᾽ Thomas Sweringin Returned his muster Role

John Evans of the company Commanded by **Capt Thomas Sweringin** ... ten shillings ... one general ....

[page 20] **Jonas Hedge** of the company Commanded by **Capt Thomas Sweringin** ... ten shillings ... one general ....

Joshua Hedge of the company Commanded by **Capt Thomas Sweringin** ... ten shillings ... one general ....

Robert Paul of the company Commanded by **Capt Thomas Sweringin** ... ten shillings ... one general ....

James Blair of the company Commanded by **Capt Thomas Sweringin** ... ten shillings ... one general ....

John Wilson of the company Commanded by **Capt Thomas Sweringin** ... ten shillings ... one general ....

George Lender of the company Commanded by **Capt Thomas Sweringin** ... ten shillings ... one general ....

William Byrns of the company Commanded by **Capt Thomas Sweringin** ... ten shillings ... one general ....

[page 20-A] **Jonah Leaman** of the company Commanded by **Capt Thomas Sweringin** ... ten shillings ... one general ....

Bartholomen Tryat of the company Commanded by **Capt Thomas Sweringin** ... ten shillings ... one general ....

John Small of the company Commanded by **Capt Thomas Sweringin** ... ten shillings ... one general ....

John Blair of the company Commanded by **Capt Thomas Sweringin** ... ten shillings ... one general ....

Mordicai Morgan of the company Commanded by **Capt Thomas Sweringin** ... ten shillings ... one general ....

Edward Morgan of the company Commanded by **Capt Thomas Sweringin** ... ten shillings ... one general ....

Abel Walker of the company Commanded by **Capt Thomas Sweringin** ... ten shillings ... one general ....

[page 21] **Samuel Harisson** of the company Commanded by **Capt Thomas Sweringin** ... ten shillings ... one general ....

Captain Thomas Speake Returned his muster Role

Henry Enoch ... thirty shilllings ... two private & one general ....

William Yates of the company Commanded by **Capt Thomas Speake** ... forty shillings ... three Private & one general ....

William Hicks of the company Commanded by **Capt Thomas Speake** ... twenty shillings ... two private ....

George Highly of the company Commanded by **Capt Thomas Speake** ... ten shillings ... one private ....

[page 21-A] **James Crabbtree** of the company Commanded by **Capt Thomas Speake** ... ten shillings ... one Private ....

John Anderson of the company Commanded by **Capt Thomas Speake** ... ten shillings ... one private ....

John George Hollingbaugh of the company Commanded by **Capt Thomas Speake** ... ten shillings ... one private ....

James Williamson of the company Commanded by **Capt Thomas Speake** ... ten shillings ... one private ....

William Bowling of the company Commanded by **Capt Thomas Speake** ... twenty shillings ... two private ....

Michael Tanner of the company Commanded by **Capt Thomas Speake** ... twenty shillings ... one private & one General ....

Stephen Russel of the company Commanded by **Capt Thomas Speake** ... twenty shillings ... one private & one general ....

[page 22] **David Brooks** of the company Commanded by **Capt Thomas Speake** ... twenty shillings ... one general & one private ....

William Lockard of the company Commanded by **Capt Thomas Speake** ... ten shillings ... one General ....

Edward Snickers of the company Commanded by **Capt Thomas Speake** ... ten shillings ... one General ....

Elisha Issaccs of the company Commanded by **Capt Thomas Speake** ... ten shillings ... one General ....

Vollentine Parkins of the company Commanded by **Capt Thomas Speake** ... ten shillings ... one General ....

John Peters of the company Commanded by **Capt Thomas Speake** ... ten shillings ... one General ....

Nicholas Perchman of the company Commanded by **Capt Thomas Speake** ... ten shillings ... one General ....

[page 22-A] **Isaac Lindsey** of the company Commanded by **Capt Thomas Speake** ... ten shillings ... one private ....

Henry Batten of the company Commanded by **Capt Thomas Speake** ... be exempt from Duty being Infirm

Captain Robert Parris Returned his Muster Role

Alexander Boyd of the company Commanded by **Capt Robert Parris** ... ten shillings ... one General ....

Richard Carter of the company Commanded by **Capt Robert Parris** ... ten shillings ... one General ....

James Craine of the company Commanded by **Capt Robert Parris** ... ten shillings ... one General ....

Robert RillGore of the company Commanded by **Capt Robert Parris** ... ten shillings ... one General ....

[page 23] **William Roberts Junr** of the company Commanded by **Capt Robert Parris** ... ten shillings ... one General ....

Edward Temmons of the company Commanded by **Capt Robert Parris** ... ten shillings ... one General ....

Robert Morgan of the company Commanded by **Capt Robert Parris** ... ten shillings ... one General ....

Richard Picket of the company Commanded by **Capt Robert Parris** ... ten shillings ... one General ....

George Hoge of the company Commanded by **Capt Robert Parris** ... ten shillings ... one General ....

Thomas Allford of the company Commanded by **Capt Robert Parris** ... ten shillings ... one General ....

Capⁿ Lewis Stephens Returned his muster Role

William Ewing of the company Commanded by **Capⁿ Lewis Stephens** ... ten shillings ... one General ....

[page 23-A] **John Snapp** of the company Commanded by **Capⁿ Lewis Stephens** ... ten shillings ... one General ....

Henry Stephens of the company Commanded by **Capⁿ Lewis Stephens** ... ten shillings ... one General ....

John Harris of the company Commanded by Cap^n Lewis Stephens ... ten shillings ... one General ....

William Curlet of the company Commanded by Cap^n Lewis Stephens ... ten shillings ... one General ....

Thomas Sharp Junr of the company Commanded by Cap^n Lewis Stephens ... ten shillings ... one General ....

George Wright Senr of the company Commanded by Cap^n Lewis Stephens ... ten shillings ... one General ....

George Wright Junr of the company Commanded by Cap^n Lewis Stephens ... ten shillings ... one General ....

Samuel Marryfield of the company Commanded by Cap^n Lewis Stephens ... ten shillings ... one General ....

[page 24] **John Foccet** [margin note is written **Fouccet**] of the company Commanded by Cap^n Lewis Stephens ... ten shillings ... one General ....

Richard Fauccet [margin note is written **Fouccet**] of the company Commanded by Cap^n Lewis Stephens ... ten shillings ... one General ....

Abraham Crissman of the company Commanded by Cap^n Lewis Stephens ... ten shillings ... one General ....

Samuel Glass of the company Commanded by Cap^n Lewis Stephens ... ten shillings ... one General ....

John Sticklor of the company Commanded by Cap^n Lewis Stephens ... ten shillings ... one General ....

George Baker of the company Commanded by Cap^n Lewis Stephens ... ten shillings ... one General ....

John North of the company Commanded by Cap^n Lewis Stephens ... ten shillings ... one General ....

On the petition of **Simon Taylor** of **Cap^n Lewis Stephens** Company Ordered that he be exempt from doing duty

Captain Henry Spear Returned his Role

Walter Cuningham of the company Commanded by **Captain Henry Spear** ... fifty shillings ... Four private & one general ....

[page 23-A] **Henry Harden** of the company Commanded by **Captain Henry Spear** ... forty shillings ... three Private & one general ....

James McCoy of the company Commanded by **Captain Henry Spear** ... thirty shilllings ... two private & one general ....

Moses McCoy of the company Commanded by **Captain Henry Spear** ... fifty Shillings ... Four private & one General ....

Zachariah McCoy... thirty shilllings ... two private & one General ....

Adam Cuningham of the company Commanded by **Captain Henry Spear** ... thirty shilllings ... two private & one general ....

Charles Ragon of the company Commanded by **Captain Henry Spear** ... twenty shilllings ... one private & one general ....

Joshua Job of the company Commanded by **Captain Henry Spear** ... fifty Shillings ... Four private & one General ....

Daniel Stover of the company Commanded by **Captain Henry Spear** ... fifty Shillings ... Four private & one General ....

John ODell of the company Commanded by **Captain Henry Spear** ... twenty shillings ... one private & one general ....

[page 25] **Robert Shirley** of the company Commanded by **Captain Henry Spear** ... twenty shillings ... one private & one general ....

Charles Thompson of the company Commanded by **Captain Henry Spear** ... thirty shilllings ... two private & one general ....

Larkin Pearpoint of the company Commanded by **Captain Henry Spear** ... forty shillings ... three Private & one general ....

Edward Cuningham of the company Commanded by **Captain Henry Spear** ... ten shillings ... one General ....

Edward Collins of the company Commanded by **Captain Henry Spear** ... ten shillings ... one General ....

William Hughes of the company Commanded by **Captain Henry Spear** ... ten shillings ... one General ....

John Daniel of the company Commanded by **Captain Henry Spear** ... ten shillings ... one General ....

William Daniel of the company Commanded by **Captain Henry Spear** ... ten shillings ... one General ....

Then the Court Adjourned till Tomorrow Eight OClock

Fairfax

[page 25-A] At a Court Martiall held for Frederick County on Satturday the 28th Day of October 1758

Present

The Right Honble **Lord Fairfaix** County Leiut
Thomas Bryan Martin Esqr Col°
John Hite, Gentleman Leiut Col°
William Vance Gentleman Major
Isace Perkins
Thomas Speake
John Funk
Thomas Swearingin		Captains
Henry Spear
Robert Paris
John Hardin

Captain **John Hardin** Returned his muster Role

John Vestall of the Company commanded by **Cap᷄ John Hardin** ... thirty shillings ... Two private & one Generall ....

John Wilson of the Company commanded by **Cap᷄ John Hardin** ... twenty shillings ... one private & one general ....

William Brown of the company commanded by **Cap᷄ John Hardin** ... thirty shillings ... two private & one general ....

George Sneed of the company commanded by **Cap᷄ John Hardin** ... thirty shillings ... two private & one general ....

[page 26] **Joseph Thomson** of the Company commanded by **Cap᷄ John Hardin** ... thirty shillings ... two private & one general ....

George Hiatt of the company commanded by **Captain John Hardin** ... ten Shillings ... one private ....

Peter Boss of the Company commanded by **Cap᷄ John Hardin** ... twenty shillings ... one private & one general ....

George Emry of the Company commanded by **Cap᷄ John Hardin** ... twenty shillings ... one private & one general ....

Isaac Thomas of the Company commanded by **Cap᷄ John Hardin** ... twenty shillings ... one private & one general ....

Freind [sic] Cox of the Company commanded by **Cap᷄ John Hardin** ... ten Shillings ... one private ....

Isaec Ealy of the Company commanded by **Cap᷄ John Hardin** ... ten Shillings ... one private ....

Jonathan Phillips of the Company commanded by **Cap᷄ John Hardin** ... thirty Shillings ... two private & one general ....

[page 26-A] **William Neil** son of **Widow Neil** of the Company commanded by **Cap᷄ John Hardin** ... ten Shillings ... one private ....

Samuel Pearsons of the Company commanded by **Cap᷄ John Hardin** ... thirty shillings ... two private & one general ....

John Humphrys of the Company commanded by **Cap᷄ John Hardin** ... thirty shillings ... two private & one general ....

Thomas Goldsberry of the Company commanded by **Cap᷄ John Hardin** ... ten Shillings ... one private ....

Simeon Hiatt of the Company commanded by **Cap᷄ John Hardin** ... thirty shillings ... two private & one general ....

Nathaniel Thomas of the Company commanded by **Cap᷄ John Hardin** ... thirty shillings ... two private & one general ....

Phillip Rheymick of the Company commanded by **Cap᷄ John Hardin** ... ten Shillings ... one general ....

Joseph Skidmore of the Company commanded by **Cap᷄ John Hardin** ... thirty shillings ... two private & one general ....

James Castles of the Company commanded by **Cap᷄ John Hardin** ... thirty shillings ... two private & one general ....

[page 27] **James Murphey** of the Company commanded by **Capt John Hardin** ... thirty shillings ... two private & one general ....

Richard Brown of the Company commanded by **Capt John Hardin** ... twenty shillings ... one private & one general ....

William Miller of the Company commanded by **Capt John Hardin** ... twenty shillings ... one private & one general ....

Solomon Burkham of the Company commanded by **Capt John Hardin** ... twenty shillings ... one private & one general ....

Benjamin Satturfield of the Company commanded by **Capt John Hardin** ... thirty shillings ... one private & one general ....

James Barret of the Company commanded by **Capt John Hardin** ... thirty shillings ... two private & one general ....

James Stedman of the Company commanded by **Capt John Hardin** ... twenty shillings ... one private & one general ....

Jacob Shovelberger of the Company commanded by **Capt John Hardin** ... twenty shillings ... one private & one general ....

Benjamin Price of the Company commanded by **Capt John Hardin** ... thirty shillings ... two private & one general ....

[page 27-A] **Daniel Newcome** of the Company commanded by **Capt John Hardin** ... twenty shillings ... one private & one general ....

Robert Harper of the Company commanded by **Capt John Hardin** ... twenty shillings ... one private & one general ....

On the Motion of **Robert Allen** of the Company Commanded by **Captain Lewis Stephens** he be discharged for the future from doing duty being above the age of Sixty Years.

Thomas Perry Lieutenant on behalf of **Captain Jacob Bowman**, Returned his Role.

William Libas of the company commanded by **Captain Jacob Bowman** ... ten Shillings ... one general ....

Thomas Cooper of the company commanded by **Captain Jacob Bowman** ... ten Shillings ... one general ....

Robert McCoy of the company commanded by **Captain Jacob Bowman** ... ten Shillings ... one general ....

William Branson of the company commanded by **Captain Jacob Bowman** ... ten Shillings ... one general ....

[page 28] **John Way** of the company commanded by **Captain Jacob Bowman** ... ten Shillings ... one general ....

Hugh Warren of the company commanded by **Captain Jacob Bowman** ... ten Shillings ... one general ....

William Husk of the company commanded by **Captain Jacob Bowman** ... ten Shillings ... one general ....

John Dyer of the company commanded by **Captain Jacob Bowman** ... ten Shillings ... one general ....

Thomas Buck of the company commanded by **Captain Jacob Bowman** ... ten Shillings ... one general ....

John Oliver of the company commanded by **Captain Jacob Bowman** ... ten Shillings ... one general ....

James Morgan of the company commanded by **Captain Jacob Bowman** ... ten Shillings ... one general ....

John Gann of the company commanded by **Captain Jacob Bowman** ... ten Shillings ... one general ....

[page 28-A] **John Lahugh** of the company commanded by **Captain Jacob Bowman** ... ten Shillings ... one general ....

Spencer Lahugh of the company commanded by **Captain Jacob Bowman** ... ten Shillings ... one general ....

Andrew MᶜCoy of the company commanded by **Captain Jacob Bowman** ... ten Shillings ... one general ....

Samuel Hasewell of the company commanded by **Captain Jacob Bowman** ... ten Shillings ... one general ....

Samuel Holliday of the company commanded by **Captain Jacob Bowman** ... ten Shillings one general ....

Charles Buck of the company commanded by **Captain Jacob Bowman** ... ten Shillings ... one general ....

Benjamin Smith of the company commanded by **Captain Jacob Bowman** ... ten Shillings ... one general ....

William Warren of the company commanded by **Captain Jacob Bowman** ... ten Shillings ... one general ....

[page 29] **William Roden** of the company commanded by **Captain Jacob Bowman** ... ten Shillings ... one general ....

Joseph Cooper of the company commanded by **Captain Jacob Bowman** ... ten Shillings ... one general ....

Ezekial Morgan of the company commanded by **Captain Jacob Bowman** ... ten Shillings ... one general ....

George Pierce of the company commanded by **Captain Jacob Bowman** ... ten Shillings one general ....

Thomas Chester of the company commanded by **Captain Jacob Bowman** ... ten Shillings ... one general ....

Issaac Hite of the company commanded by **Captain Jacob Bowman** ... ten shillings ... one general ....

Caleb Powell of the company commanded by **Captain Jacob Bowman** ... ten shillings ... one general ....

William Miller Gent of the company commanded by **Captain Jacob Bowman** ... ten Shillings ... one general ....

Lewis Selser of the company commanded by **Captain Jacob Bowman** ... ten Shillings ... one general ....

[page 29-A] **Robert Halfpenny** of the company commanded by **Captain Jacob Bowman** ... ten Shillings ... one general ....

Captain John Funk Returned his muster Role

Theobald Fight of the company commanded by **Captain John Funk** ... ten Shillings ... one private ....

Captain John Denton ... Five pounds ... one General muster & a Court Martial within Twelve Months Last past

Archebald Ruddle Lieutenant ... twenty shillings ... one general ....

Captain Isaac Parkins Returned his muster Role

Peter Helfenstone of the Commanded by **Captain Isaac Parkins** ... twenty shillings ... two private ....

John Stewart of the company commanded by **Captain Isaac Parkins** ... ten Shillings ... one private ....

Lawrence Hough of the Company commanded by **Captain Isaac Parkins** ... twenty shillings ... two private ....

[page 30] **John Hainy** of the Company commanded by **Captain Isaac Parkins** ... thirty shillings ... three private ....

Henry Summer of the Company commanded by **Captain Isaac Parkins** ... twenty shillings ... two private ....

John Shmearer of the Company commanded by **Captain Isaac Parkins** ... ten Shillings ... one private ....

Frederick Conrod of the Company commanded by **Captain Isaac Parkins** ... ten Shillings ... one private ....

Matthias Calmon of the Company commanded by **Captain Isaac Parkins** ... twenty shillings ... two private ....

Martin Proston of the Company commanded by **Captain Isaac Parkins** ... ten Shillings ... one private ....

John Adam of the Company commanded by **Captain Isaac Parkins** ... twenty shillings ... two private ....

Thomas Brook of the Company commanded by **Captain Isaac Parkins** ... twenty shillings ... two private ....

John Peters of the Company commanded by **Captain Isaac Parkins** ... ten Shillings one private ....

[page 30-A] **Paul Peters** of the Company commanded by **Captain Isaac Parkins** ... ten Shillings ... one private ....

Anthony Moore of the Company commanded by **Captain Isaac Parkins** ... thirty shillings ... three private ....

Joseph Horner of the Company commanded by **Captain Isaac Parkins** ... thirty shillings ... three private ....

Thomas Berry of the Company commanded by **Captain Isaac Parkins** ... ten Shillings ... one private ....

James Clarke of the Company commanded by **Captain Isaac Parkins** ... forty shillings ... four private ....

Thomas M'Clon of the Company commanded by **Captain Isaac Parkins** ... twenty shillings ... two private ....

Alexander Brady of the Company commanded by **Captain Isaac Parkins** ... fifty shillings ... four private & one general ....

Thomas Leadsome of the Company commanded by **Captain Isaac Parkins** ... twenty shillings ... two private ....

Henry Messersmith of the Company commanded by **Captain Isaac Parkins** ... twenty shillings ... two private ....

[page 31] **George Thompson** of the Company commanded by **Captain Isaac Parkins** ... twenty shillings ... two private ....

Julias Spiker of the Company commanded by **Captain Isaac Parkins** ... ten Shillings ... one private ....

Phillip Bush of the Company commanded by **Captain Isaac Parkins** ... ten Shillings ... one private ....

Everhart Dearing of the Company commanded by **Captain Isaac Parkins** ... ten Shillings ... one private ....

Peter Meisemore of the Company commanded by **Captain Isaac Parkins** ... thirty shillings ... two private & one general ....

Pauleer Faw of the Company commanded by **Captain Isaac Parkins** ... ten Shillings ... one private ....

Lewis Hough of the Company commanded by **Captain Isaac Parkins** ... ten Shillings ... one private ....

George Shade of the Company commanded by **Captain Isaac Parkins** ... ten Shillings ... one private ....

[page 31-A] **Abraham Bayly** of the Company commanded by **Captain Isaac Parkins** ... ten Shillings ... one private ....

Anthony Taviner of the Company commanded by **Captain Isaac Parkins** ... forty shillings ... three private & one general ....

Handell Denny of the Company commanded by **Captain Isaac Parkins** ... ten Shillings ... one private ....

William Gilham of the Company commanded by **Captain Isaac Parkins** ... ten Shillings ... one private ....

Robert Milbourn of the Company commanded by **Captain Isaac Parkins** ... thirty shillings ... three private ....

John Bryan of the Company commanded by **Captain Isaac Parkins** ... thirty shillings ... two private & one general ....

Samuel Young of the Company commanded by **Captain Isaac Parkins** ... ten Shillings ... one private ....

William Burrows of the Company commanded by **Captain Isaac Parkins** ... ten Shillings ... one private ....

Thomas Lossly of the Company commanded by **Captain Isaac Parkins** ... ten Shillings ... one private ....

[page 32] **William Shaine** of the Company commanded by **Captain Isaac Parkins** ... ten Shillings ... one private ....

Thomas Doran of the Company commanded by **Captain Isaac Parkins** ... ten Shillings ... one private ....

Robert Jackson of the Company commanded by **Captain Isaac Parkins** ... ten Shillings ... one private ....

Henry Shoemaker of the Company commanded by **Captain Isaac Parkins** ... ten Shillings ... one private ....

Peter Perry of the Company commanded by **Captain Isaac Parkins** ... ten Shillings ... one private ....

George Sell of the Company commanded by **Captain Isaac Parkins** ... ten Shillings ... one private ....

Tobias Otto of the Company commanded by **Captain Isaac Parkins** ... ten Shillings ... one private ....

Phillip Helfenstone of the Company commanded by **Captain Isaac Parkins** ... ten Shillings ... one private ....

Francis Collins of the Company commanded by **Captain Isaac Parkins** ... ten Shillings ... one private ....

[page 32-A] **Meoly Vagan** of the Company commanded by **Captain Isaac Parkins** ... ten Shillings ... one private ....

Phillip Babb Junr of the Company commanded by **Captain Isaac Parkins** ... thirty shillings ... two private & one general ....

James Williams of the Company commanded by **Captain Isaac Parkins** ... ten Shillings ... one private ....

James Hagen of the Company commanded by **Captain Isaac Parkins** ... ten Shillings ... one private ....

William Phillips of the Company commanded by **Captain Isaac Parkins** ... ten Shillings ... one private ....

Ordered that Mr Isaac Parkins be Continued Treasurer to receive & dispose of the Several Sums by him Received of the Sheriff as he Shall be ordered by this Court from time to time

Ordered that the Clerk dilver the Several orders of this Court Martial to the Sheriff

Ordered that the Sheriff Receive & Collect the Several Fines Inflicted by this Court Martial & pay the Same to the Treasurer According to Law

Ordered that the Treasurer Accoumpt for the Several Sums Arising from the Several fines which he Shall Receive of the Sheriff at the next Court Martial or when he Shall be thereunto Required

Ordered that the Treasurer pay the Clerk Ten Pounds out of the fines Inflicted by this Court Martial as his Sallery

Fairfax

[handwriting changes]
[page 33] At a Court Martial Held for Frederick County on Fryday the 31st
of October 1760

Present

John Hite Colonel
Lewis Stephen Major
Lewis Moore
Thomas Sweringin
John Allen
Joseph McDowell
John Denton
Henry Spear   Captains
Van Sweringin
Cornelias Ruddle
Marques Callimese
John Griendfield
Thomas Speke
John Bowman
Isaac Parkins

Captain Lewis Moore Returned his roll
John Simpson Corperal of the Company Commanded by **Cap^n Lewis
Moore** ... two Shillings for appearing without ammunition at one Private
muster ....
John Arnold Corperal in the Company Commanded by **Cap^n Lewis Moore**
be discharged from doing further Duty at Musters (on his Pitioning)
James Dorster of the Company Commanded by **Cap^n Lewis Moore** ... ten
shillings ... one private ....
John Crumbley of the Company Commanded by **Cap^n Lewis Moore** ... forty
shillings ... three private & one general ....
Thomas Martin of the Company Commanded by **Cap^n Lewis Moore** ... forty
shillings ... three private & one general ....
Jacob Moon of the Company Commanded by **Cap^n Lewis Moore** ... forty
shillings ... three private & one general ....
[page 33-A] **Aaron Hackney** of the Company Commanded by **Cap^n Lewis
Moore**... forty shillings ... three private & one general ....
James Dunbarr of the Company Commanded by **Cap^n Lewis Moore** ... forty
shillings ... three private & one general ....
William Dorster of the Company Commanded by **Cap^n Lewis Moore** ... ten
shillings ... one private ....
John Handshaw of the Company Commanded by **Cap^n Lewis Moore** ... forty
shillings ... three private & one general ....

Abraham Low of the Company Commanded by Cap^n **Lewis Moore** ... ten shillings ... one private ....

Patrick Dooly of the Company Commanded by Cap^n **Lewis Moore** ... ten shillings ... one private ... & two Shillings for apppearing at a muster without amunition ....

Patrick Towland of the Company Commanded by **Captain Lewis Moore** on his Motion be discharged from Further duty at Musters

Thomas Fletcher of the Company Commanded by Cap^n **Lewis Moore** ... ten shillings ... one private ....

John Barrett of the Company Commanded by Cap^n **Lewis Moore** ... forty shillings ... three private & one general ....

James Barret of the Company Commanded by Cap^n **Lewis Moore** ... forty shillings ... three private & one general ....

Jacob Barret of the Company Commanded by Cap^n **Lewis Moore** ... forty shillings ... three private & one general ....

[page 34] **Thomas Brumfield** of the Company Commanded by Cap^n **Lewis Moore** ... two shillings for appearing at one private muster without ammunition ....

Luke Dillon of the Company Commanded by Cap^n **Lewis Moore** ... forty shillings ... three private & one general ....

Peter Ruble of the Company Commanded by Cap^n **Lewis Moore** ... forty shillings ... three private & one general ....

Samuel Ruble of the Company Commanded by Cap^n **Lewis Moore** ... ten shillings ... one private ....

Benjamin Barrett of the Company Commanded by Cap^n **Lewis Moore** ... thirty Shillings ... two private & one general ....

Richard Ridgway of the Company Commanded by Cap^n **Lewis Moore** ... forty shillings ... three private & one general ....

Josiah Ridgway of the Company Commanded by Cap^n **Lewis Moore** ... forty shillings ... three private & one general ....

Richard Ridgway of the Company Commanded by Cap^n **Lewis Moore** ... forty shillings ... three private & one general ....

[page 34-A] **William Jolliff Junr** of the Company Commanded by Cap^n **Lewis Moore** ... forty shillings ... three private & one general ....

Thomas Berry of the Company Commanded by Cap^n **Lewis Moore** ... forty shillings ... three private & one general ....

William Reece of the Company Commanded by Cap^n **Lewis Moore** ... forty shillings ... three private & one general ....

Edmond Jolliff of the Company Commanded by Cap^n **Lewis Moore** ... forty shillings ... three private & one general ....

James Ballinger of the Company Commanded by Cap^n **Lewis Moore** ... forty shillings ... three private & one general ....

Josiah Ballinger of the Company Commanded by **Cap^n Lewis Moore** ... forty shillings ... three private & one general ....

Alexander Ross of the Company Commanded by **Cap^n Lewis Moore** ... forty shillings ... three private & one general ....

Isaac Folles of the Company Commanded by **Cap^n Lewis Moore** ... forty shillings ... three private & one general ....

Thomas Dorster of the Company Commanded by **Cap^n Lewis Moore** ... ten shillings ... one private ....

John Davis of the Company Commanded by **Cap^n Lewis Moore** ... ten shillings ... one private ....

[page 35] Ordered that the Collector Repay to **James Clark** of the Company Commanded by **Captain Isaac Parkins** the sum of twenty Shillings part of forty Shillings which he was fined the 28th Day of October 1758

Ordered that **Archabald Ruddell** be Repaid the sum of twenty Shillings by the Treasurer which he was fined the 28th day of October 1758

Ordered that **Alexander Boyd** be Repaid by the Teasurer ten Shillings which he was fined the [blank] Day of October 1758

Ordered that the Treasurer Repay to **Robert Hodgson** fifteen Shillings which he was fined in the year 1755

Ordered that the Treasurer Repay to **Captain John Denton** the Sum of Five pounds which he was fined the [blank] Day of October 1758

Ordered that the Treasurer Repay to **Henry Mercer Smith** twenty Shillings which he was fined the [blank] Day of October 1758

Ordered that the Treasurer Repay to **Henry Stephens** ten Shillings which he was fined the [blank] day of October 1758.

On the motion of **Major Lewis Stephens & Captain John Allen** on behalf of **Henry Stephens**

Ordered that the said **Henry Stephens** be discharged from further Duty at Musters

Ordered that **John Evans** of the Company Commanded by **Captain Thomas Sweringin** (on his Motioning) be discharged from farther Duty at Musters

Ordered that **Edward Carder** of the Company Commanded by **Captain Marques Calimese** (on his Motioning) be discharged from further Duty at Musters

Ordered that **Duggel Campbell** of the Company Commanded by **Captain Thomas Sweringins** (on his Motioning be discharged from farther Duty at Musters

Ordered that **George Anman** of the Company Commanded by **Captain John Funk** (on his Motioning) be discharged from further Duty at Musters

[page 35-A] Ordered that **John Beckett** of the Company Commanded by **Captain John Allen** (on his Motion be discharged from farther Duty at

Ordered that **Daniel Sutherland** of the Company Commanded by **Captain Allen** (on his Motion) be discharged from farther Duty at Musters

Ordered that **William Russell** of the Company Commanded by **Captain Joseph McDowell** (on his Motion) be discharged from farther Duty at Musters

Ordered that **Jacob Cockley** of the Company Commanded by **Captain John Allen** (on his Motion) be discharged from further duty at Musters

Ordered that **John Frederick Fon Feigh Helm** [margin note written **Feigh Helm**] of the Company Commanded by **Captain Joseph McDowell** (on his Motion) be discharged from Further duty at Musters

Ordered that **Nicholas Rinuller** [margin note written **Rionuller**] of the Company Commanded by **Captain John Allen** (on his Motion) be discharged from further duty at Musters

Ordered that **Stephen Hotzenbeller** of the Company Commanded by **Captn John Allen** (on his Motion) be discharged from further duty at Musters

Ordered that **Henry Perrygoy** of the Company Commanded by **Captain Van Sweringin** (on his Motion) be discharged from further duty at Musters

Ordered that **John Niecwanger** of the Company Commanded by **Captain Joseph McDowell** (on his Motion) be discharged from further duty at Musters

Ordered that **John Larack** of the Company Commanded by **Captain Jospeh McDowell** (on his Motion) be discharged from further duty at Musters

Ordered that **Wm Evans** of the Company Commanded by **Captain Joseph McDowell** (on his Motion) be discharged from further duty at Musters

Ordered that **Zebulon Tharp** of the Company Commanded by **Captain John Allen** (on his Motion) be discharged from further duty at Musters

Ordered that **Peter Wilt** of the Company Commanded by **Captain Isaac Parkins** (on his Motion) be discharged from further duty at Musters

[page 36] Ordered that **Frederick Rantz** of the Company Commanded by **Cap^n Isaac Parkins** (on his Motion) be discharged from further duty at Musters

Ordered that **Henry Rinker** of the Company Commanded by **Captain Isaac Parkins** (on his Motion) be discharged from further Duty at Musters

Ordered that **William Miller** Gent of the Company Commanded by **Captain John Bowman** (on his Motion) be Discharged from further duty at Musters

Ordered that the Treasurer repay to **William Byrns** the Sum of ten Shillings which he was fined October 1758

Captain Ruddle ... Five pounds for Failing to bring his Company into the field at the Last Generall muster & Failing to make a proper Return According to Law

Captain John Scheene [Skene in margin] ... Five pounds for Failing to appear with his Company at the Last Generall ....

Captain Thomas Caton ... Five pounds for Failing to appear with his Company at the Last Generall Muster

Captain Marquis Calmese returned his muster Roll

John Painter of the company commanded by **Captain Marquis Calmese** ... twenty shillings ... one private & one Generall ....

Thomas Burrage of the Company Commanded **Captain Calemese** (On his Motion) be Discharged from further Duty at Musters

William Berry of the company commanded by **Captain Marquis Calemese** ... ten shillings ... one private ....

[page 36-A] **George Jameson** of the company commanded by **Captain Marquis Calemese** ... twenty shillings ... one private & one general ....

Robert Painter of the company commanded by **Captain Marquis Calemese** ... twenty shillings ... one private & one general ....

Samuel Humbar of the company commanded by **Captain Marquis Calemese** ... twenty shillings ... one private & one general ....

Thomas Howell of the company commanded by **Captain Marquis Calemese** ... ten shillings ... one private ....

James Huston of the company commanded by **Captain Marquis Calemese** ... ten shillings ... one private ....

John Rout of the company commanded by **Captain Marquis Calemese** ... ten shillings ... one general ....

Edward Rodgers of the company commanded by **Captain Marquis Calemese** ... ten shillings ... one general ....

John Painter of the company commanded by **Captain Marquis Calemese** ... ten shillings ... one general ....

[page 37] **Robert Hains** of the company commanded by **Captain Marquis Calemese** ... ten shillings ... one general ....

Thomas Branson of the company commanded by **Captain Marquis Calemese** ... ten shillings ... one general ....

John Arnold of the company commanded by **Captain Marquis Calemese** ... ten shillings ... one general ....

Alexander Oglevey of the company commanded by **Captain Marquis Calemese** ... ten shillings ... one general ....

Benjah Grubbs of the company commanded by **Captain Marquis Calemese** ... ten shillings ... one general ....

William Wood of the company commanded by **Captain Marquis Calemese** ... ten shillings ... one general ....

Captain John Funk ... ten pounds for failing to make a proper Return of those that have not appeared at his Private Musters & of those that have failed to appear with Arms Powder & Ball within Twelve Months last past

Jacob Miller of the Company Commanded by **Captain John Denton** ... forty Shillings ... three private & one general ....

Abraham Miller of the Company Commanded by **Captain John Denton** ...
fifty shillings ... four private & one general ....

[page 37-A] **Francis Weigell** of the Company Commanded by **Captain John
Denton** ... fifty shillings ... four private & one general ....

Robert Lemen of the Company Commanded by **Captain Van Sweringin** ...
ten shillings ... one general ....

Alexander Lemen of the Company Commanded by **Captain Van
Sweringin** ... two shillings for failing to appear with his Proper arms &
Ammunition ....

Thomas Bright of the Company Commanded by **Captain Van Sweringin** ...
twenty shillings ... one private & one general ....

William Forster of the Company Commanded by **Captain Van Sweringin** ...
ten shillings ... one private ....

Nicholas Parker of the Company Commanded by **Captain Van Sweringin** ...
twenty shillings ... one private & one general ....

Then the Court Adjourned till Tomorrow morning Eight oclock

Jn° Hite

[page 38] At a Court Martial Held for Frederick County on Satterday the
First Day of November 1760

Present

John Hite Colonel		
Lewis Stephens Major		
John Grienfield	**Isaac Parkins**	
Thomas Sweringin	**John Denton**	
Van Sweringin	**John Bowman**	Captains
Thomas Speke	**Henry Spear**	
John Allen	**Lewis Moore**	

Captain Henry Speake Returned his Roll

James McCoy of the Company Commanded by **Captain Henry Spear** ... fifty
shilling ... four private & one general ....

Henry Hardin of the Company Commanded by **Captain Henry Speake** ...
fifty shillings ... four private & one general ....

Walter Cunningham of the Company Commanded by **Captain Henry
Spear** ... fifty shillings ... four private & one general ....

Moses McCoy of the Company Commanded by **Captain Henry Spear** ... fifty
shillings ... four private & one general ....

[page 38-A] **Zacheriah McCoy** of the Company Commanded by **Captain
Henry Spear** ... fifty shillings ... four private & one general ....

Adam Cunningham of the Company Commanded by **Captain Henry
Spear** ... fifty shillings ... four private & one general ....

On the motion of **James Ireson** on behalf of **John Hankins** of **Captain
Henry Spears** Company

Ordered that the said **Hankins** be discharged from doing further Duty at Musters

Daniel Stover of the Company Commanded by **Captain Henry Spear** ... fifty shillings ... four private & one general ....

Larkin Pearpoint of the Company Commanded by **Captain Henry Speke** [sic] ... fifty shillings ... four private & one general ....

Samuel Stover of the Company Commanded by **Captain Henry Spear** ... fifty shillings ... four private & one general ....

On the motion of **Captain Henry Spear** on behalf of **Joshua Job** its ordered that the said Job be discharged from doing further Duty at muster ....

Thomas Hume of the Company Commanded by **Captain Henry Spere** ... twenty shillings ... two private ....

[page 39] **David Hume** of the Company Commanded by **Captain Henry Spear** ... thirty shillings ... two private & one general ....

John Allen sen of the Company Commanded by **Captain Henry Spear** ... ten shillings ... one general ....

William Sevier of the Company Commanded by **Captain Henry Spear** ... twenty shillings ... one private & one general ....

John Hurt of the Company Commanded by **Captain Henry Spear** ... twenty shillings ... one private & one general ....

Reubin Padgett of the Company Commanded by **Captain Henry Spear** ... ten shillings ... one general ....

James McNiel of the Company Commanded by **Captain Henry Spear** ... ten shillings ... one general ....

[page 39-A] **Macksamelaon Bush** of the Company Commanded by **Captain Henry Spear** ... twenty shillings ... one private & one general ....

Edmond Collens of the Company Commanded by **Captain Henry Spear** ... ten shillings ... one general ....

James Collins of the Company Commanded by **Captain Henry Spear** ... ten shillings ... one general ....

William Daniel of the Company Commanded by **Captain Henry Spear** (on his motion) be discharged from further duty at musters

Georg Bethell of the Company Commanded by **Captain Henry Spear** ... ten shillings ... one general ....

James Sisk of the Company Commanded by **Captain Henry Spear** ... ten shillings ... one general ....

Richard Harmond of the Company Commanded by **Captain Henry Spear** ... ten shillings ... one general ....

John Lacy Corpral in the Company Commanded by **Captain Henry Spear** ... ten shillings ... one private ....

Thomas Lemen of the Company Commanded by **Capⁿ John Griendfield** ... Five pounds for Accepting a Lieutenants Commission in the said Company & not Serving in the same within Three months last past [page 40] **Phillip Bush** of the Company Commanded by **Captain John Griendfield** ... Five pounds for Accepting an Ensigns Commission in the said Company & failing to serve in the same within three months of the time he did accept the same

Joshua Baker of the Company Commanded by **Captain John Griendfield** ... forty shillings ... four private ....

John Campbell of the Company Commanded by **Captain John Grienfield** ... thirty shillings ... three private ....

Samuel Young of the Company Commanded by **Captain John Grienfield** ... thirty shillings ... three private ....

Daniel Bush of the Company Commanded by **Captain John Grienfield** ... thirty shillings ... three private ....

Henry Brinker of the Company Commanded by **Captain John Grienfield** ... thirty shillings ... three private ....

Thomas Smith of the Company Commanded by **Captain John Grienfield** ... thirty shillings ... three private ....

[page 40-A] **Andrew Fridly** of the Company Commanded by **Captain John Grienfield** ... thirty shillings ... three private ....

Adam Haymaker of the Company Commanded by **Captain John Grienfield** ... twenty shillings ... two private ....

George Shade of the Company Commanded by **Captain John Grienfield** ... twenty shillings ... two private ....

Laurance Huff of the Company Commanded by **Captain John Grienfield** ... twenty shillings ... two private ....

Nicholas Shrock of the Company Commanded by **Captain John Grienfield** ... thirty shillings ... three private ....

Matthias Colman of the Company Commanded by **Captain John Grienfield** ... thirty shillings ... three private ....

Christopher Aldred of the Company Commanded by **Captain John Grienfield** ... twenty shillings ... two private ....

James Hoge of the Company Commanded by **Captain John Grienfield** ... 12 shillings for appearing at one private & One General musters without Arms & Ammunition ....

John Stuart of the Company Commanded by **Captain Isaac Parkins** ... forty shillings ... three private & one general ....

[page 41] On the motion of **Captain Van Sweringin** on behalf of **John Pierce** its ordered that the said **Pierce** be discharged from further duty at Musters

On the motion of **Captain Van Sweringin** on behalf of **Anthony Turner** Ordered that the said **Turner** be discharged from further duty at musters

John Allen Serg^t present of the Company Commanded by **Cap^n Robert Peariss** be discharged from that s^d Company & that he muster for the future under **Captain John Allen**

Thomas Love of the Company Commanded by **Captain Robert Pearriss** ... ten shillings ... one private ....

William Roberts of the Company Commanded by **Captain Robert Peariss** ... twenty shillings ... one private & one general ....

John Bell of the Company Commanded by **Captain Robert Pearriss** ... ten shillings ... one private ....

Robert Morgan of the Company Commanded by **Captain Robert Pearriss** ... ten shillings ... one private ....

John Williams of the Company Commanded by **Captain Robert Pearriss** ... ten shillings ... one private ....

[page 41-A] **Richard Johnston** of the Company Commanded by **Captain Robert Pearriss** ... ten shillings ... one private ....

On the motion of Mr **William Callimese** on behalf of **Jeremiah Redmon** Ordered that the said **Redmon** be discharged from farther Duty at musters

Thomas Williams of the Company Commanded by **Captain Robert Pearriss** ... ten shillings ... one private ....

Daniel Kelleh of the Company Commanded by **Captain Robert Pearriss** ... ten shillings ... one general ....

Samuel Poore of the Company Commanded by **Captain Robert Pearriss** ... ten shillings ... one private ....

Benjamin Smith of the Company Commanded by **Captain Robert Pearriss** ... ten shillings ... one general ....

Nathaniel McConnell of the Company Commanded by **Captain Robt Pearriss** ... ten shillings ... one general ....

Nathaniel Curry of the Company Commanded by **Captain Robert Peariss** ... ten shillings ... one general ....

Moses Welton of the Company Commanded by **Captain Thomas Speke** ... ten shillings ... one private ....

[page 42] **Thomas Hill** of the Company Commanded by **Captain Thomas Speke** ... twenty shillings ... two private ....

Edward Chapman of the Company Commanded by **Captain Thomas Speke** ... ten shillings ... one private ....

John Masterson of the Company Commanded by **Captain Thomas Speke** ... thirty shillings ... three private ....

Francis Niel of the Company Commanded by **Captain Thomas Speke** ... forty shillings ... three private & one general ....

Charles Lowry of the Company Commanded by **Captain Thomas Speke** ... ten shillings ... one private ....

William Johnstone of the Company Commanded by **Captain Thos Speke** ... thirty shillings ... three private ....

Benjamin Harrisson of the Company Commanded by **Captain Thos Speke** ... thirty shillings ... two private & one general ....

Samuel Mason of the Company Commanded by **Captain Thomas Speke** ... ten shillings ... one private ....

[page 42-A] **John Logan** of the Company Commanded by **Captain Thomas Speke** ... ten shillings ... one private ....

John Percles of the Company Commanded by **Captain Thomas Speke** ... thirty shillings ... two private & one general ....

James Mercer of the Company Commanded by **Captain Thomas Speke** ... twenty shillings ... one private & one general ....

Michael Cravens of the Company Commanded by **Captain Thomas Speke** ... ten shillings ... one private ....

Wm Cook of the Company Commanded by **Captain Thomas Speke** ... ten shillings ... one general ....

Ordered that **Mr John Grienfield** be appointed Treasurer to receive & Dispose of the several sums by him Received of the Sheriff as he shall be ordered by this Court from time to time

Ordered that the Clarke [sic] diliver the Several orders of this Court Martial to the Sheriff

Ordered that the Sheriff Receive the Several orders of this Court Martial of the Clark & Collect the Several fines imposed in these orders & pay the same to the Treasuerer according to Law.

[page 43] Ordered that the Treasurer Account for the sum arrising from the Several fines which he shall Receive of the Sheriff at the next Court Martial or when he shall be thereunto Required

Ordered that the Sheriff pay to **Robert Rutherford** Clarke the sum of Twelve pounds out of the fines Inflicted by this Court Martial as his Sallery for services at this Court Martial

Ordered that the Treasurer Repay to the Several Captains that have advanced Cash to Buy Drums & other Necessary Trophies for their Respective Companys the sums that they have advanced for that purpose on their producing a fair & Legal account & further that he purchase Drums & other necissarys for the Several Remaining Companys as far as the Cash that he Receives of the Sheriff will purchase after paying the firs mentioned Sums

Ordered that the sheriff have Two pounds ten shillings for attending the Court Martial & that this order shall be good for so much when he settles with the Treasurer

Then the court adjourned till the next Court Martial

Jn Hite

[page 43-A] At a Court martial Held for Frederick County on Fryday the 9th Day of October 1761

Present

John Hite Esqr Col°
Lewis Stephens Esqr Maj^r
Van Sweringin
Thomas Caton
John Funk
Robert Pearis
Thomas Sweringin
Lewis Moore   Gent Captains
Thomas Speak
John Allen
John Greenfield
Joseph McDowell
Marquis Calmese
John Denton
John Schene

On the the Motion of **Phillip Bush**
Ordered that the fine (which was laid on him at the last Court martial for not Swearing into a Lieutenants Commission being Five pounds) be repaid him by the Treasurer

On the motion of **Nicholas Shrock**
Ordered that the Treasuerer repay him the fine laid on him at the last Court martial for failing to under **Capt John Greenfield** the said fine being thirty shillings

On the motion of **Alexander Ross**
Ordered that he be repaid by the Tresurer the same fine that was inflicted on him at the last Court Martial for not mustering under **Capt Lewis Moore**

[page 44] On the motion of **Nicholas Parker**
Ordered that the Treasurer remit to him the same fine that was inflicted on him at the last Court Martial for not mustering under **Capt Van Sweringin**

On the motion of **Capt John Funk**
Ordered that the Treasurer repay him ten pounds which he was fined at the last Court Martial

On the motion of **Henry Brinker**
Ordered that the Treasurer repay him the same fine that was inflicted on him at the last Court Martial for not mustering under **Capt John Greenfield** being thirty Shillings

On the motion of **James McNeal** of **Capt Henry Spears** Company

Ordered that the Treasurer repay him the same Sum which was inflicted on
him at the last Court Martial
On the motion of **Adam Haymaker** of **Capt John Greenfields** Company
Ordered that the Treasurer repay him the same Sum inflicted on him at the
last Court Martial
On the Motion of **Christopher Heskell** of **Capt John Greenfields** Company
Ordered that the Treasurer repay him the same fine Inflicted on him at the
last Court Martial
On the motion of **Capt Thomas Caton**
Ordered that the Treasurer repay him the same Sum inflicted on him at the
last Court Martial
[page 44-A] It appearing to the Court Martial that the fine laid on **Laurance
Hoof** is Eregular
Ordered that the Treasurer repay the same to him the s^d fine being inflicted
on him at the last Court Martial for not mustering under **Capt John
Greenfield**
George Farrar Ensign in **Capt Marquis Calmese** Company ... ten shillings
for appearing at the Last General not Accoutered as the law directs
Benjamin Berry Lieut. of **Capt Thomas Speaks** Company ... ten shil^{gs} [sic]
for not appearing Accoutered at the last General as the Law directs
On the motion of **Edward Rodgers** of **Capt Marques Calmese**'s Company
Ordered that the Treasurer repay him the same fine inflicted on him at the
last Court Martial
George Corker of the Company Commanded by **Capt Van Sweringin** ... ten
shillings ... one private ....
Adam Oler of the Company Commanded by **Capt Van Sweringin** ... ten
shillings ... one private ....
Isaac Morgan of the Company Commanded by **Capt Van Sweringin** ... ten
shillings ... last general muster
[page 45] **Benjamin Sanders** of the Company Commanded by **Capt Van
Sweringin** ... ten shillings ... the last general muster
Ralf Withers of the Company Commanded by **Capt John Bowman** be
discharged of further Duty at musters
On the motion of **James Vance** of the Company Commanded by **Capt
Joseph McDowell**
he be discharged of further duty at Musters
Michael Humble (of the Company Commanded by **Capt Joseph McDowell**
on his Motion) be discharged of further duty at Musters
Ordered **Isaac McCuing** (of **Capt Joseph McDowells** Company) on his
Motion be discharged of further duty at Musters
Phillip Glass (of **Capt John Funks** Company on his Motion) be discharged
of further duty at Musters

Martin Black (of **Capt John Funks** Company on his Motion) be discharged of further duty at Musters

John Fleming (of **Capt John Funs** [sic] Company on his Motion) be discharged of further duty at Musters

Rynard Bodden (of **Capt John Funks** Company on his Motion) be discharged of further duty at Musters

Geroge Weaver (of **Capt John Funks** Company on his Motion) be discharged of further duty at Musters

Richard Folio (of **Capt John Bowmans** Company on his Motion) be discharged of further duty at Musters

[page 45-A] **Charles Huddle** (of **Captain John Funks** Company) be discharged of further Duty at Musters

Edward Reed (of **Capt Robert Pearis's** Company on his Motion) be discharged of Further duty at Musters

Dennis Bow (of **Capt Marques Calmese** Company on his Motion) be discharged of Further duty at Musters

James Henry (of **Capt Marques Calmese's** Company on his Motion) be discharged of Further duty at Musters

John Lacy (of **Capt Henry Spears** Company on his Motion) be discharged of further duty at Musters

William Seveer (of **Capt Henry Spears** Company on his Motion) be discharged of further duty at Musters

John Ammet (of **Capt William Crawfords** Company on his Motion) be discharged of further duty at Musters

Thomas Goldsberry (of **Capt William Crawfords** Company on the s^d Captains Motion) be discharged of further duty at Musters

John Hartly (of **Captain William Crawfords** Company on the Motion of the s^d Captain) be discharged of further duty at Musters

Charles Barns (of **Captain John Allens** Company on his Motion) be discharged of further duty at Musters

William Overhall (of **Captain Henry Spears** Company on his Motion) be discharged of further duty at Musters

Joseph Abell (of **Captain Henry Spears** Company on the Motion of **Abram Killer** L^t) be discharged of further duty at Musters

[page 46] **William Whitson** (of **Capt Henry Spears** Company on the Motion of **Abraham Killer** L^t) be discharged of further duty at Musters

Darby McCarty (of **Capt Henry Spears** Company on the Motion of **Abraham Killer** L^t) be discharged of further duty at Musters

Barnaby Hagan (of **Capt Henry Spears** Company on the Motion of **Abraham Keller** L^t) be discharged of further duty at Musters

James Hogg (of **Capt Joseph McDowells** Company on the Motion of the s^d Capt) be discharged of further duty at Musters

Henry Netherton (of Capt Henry Spears Company on the Motion of Lieu^t Abram Killer) is discharged from further duty at Musters

George McKenny (of Capt Lewis Moores Company on his Motion) be discharged of further duty at Musters

John Chinnoath (of Capt Lewis Moores Company on the Motion of the s^d Captain) be discharged of further duty at Musters

William Chinnoath (of Capt Lewis Moores Company on the Motion of the s^d Captain) be discharged from further duty at Musters

Thomas Martin (of Capt Lewis Moores Company at Motion of s^d Capt) be discharged of further duty at Musters

William Lodwith (of Capt Thomas Speaks Company on the Motion the s^d Capt) be discharged of further duty at Musters

[page 46-A] Enos Thomas (of Capt Lewis Moores Company on the Motion of the said Captain) be discharged of further duty at Musters

William Dillon (of Capt Lewis Moores Company on the Motion of the s^d Captain) be discharged of further duty at Musters

Mark Iler (of Capt Cornelias Ruddles Company on his Motion) be discharged of further duty at Musters

Thomas Postgate (of Capt Marquise Calmese Company on his Motion) be discharged of further duty at Musters

Edward Rogers (of Capt Marquise Callimes's Company on his Motion) be discharged of further duty at Musters

Robert Morgan (of Capt Robert Pearis's Company being in some measure blind or near sighted) be discharged of further Duty at Musters

William Boggs (of Capt Thomas Caton's Company on the Motion of the s^d Captain) be discharged of further duty at Musters

William Dobbin (on the Motion of Robert Rutherford) be discharged of further duty at Musters

William Chambers (of Capt John Allens Company on the Motion of the s^d Capt) be discharged of further duty at Musters

Jacob Tzitzir (of Capt John Funks Company on the Motion of the s^d Captain) be discharged of further duty at Musters

Leuit^t Stephen Rowlings of Capt Thomas Catons Company ... twenty shillings ... the last General ....

[page 47] William Cherry of Capt Thomas Catons Company ... ten Shillings ... the last General ....

John Mercer of Capt Thomas Catons Company ... ten Shillings ... the last General ....

Josiah Hultz of Capt Thomas Cantons Company ... ten Shillings ... the last General ....

Adam Pain of Capt Thomas Cantons Company ... ten Shillings ... the last General ....

James Jack of Capt Thomas Cantons Company ... ten Shillings ... the last General ....

Jacob Johnston of Capt Thomas Cantons Company ... ten Shillings ... the last General ....

John Cherry of Capt Thos Catons Company ... ten Shillings ... the last General ....

James Logan of Capt Thomas Cantons Company ... ten Shillings ... the last General ....

Thomas Applegate of Capt Thomas Cantons Company ... ten Shillings ... the last General ....

George Pack of Capt Thos Catons Company ... ten Shillings ... the last General ....

Samuel Pack of Capt Thomas Cantons Company ... ten Shillings ... the last General ....

Thomas Pack of Capt Thos Catons Company ... ten Shillings ... the last General ....

[page 47-A] William Noble of Capt Thomas Cantons Company ... ten Shillings ... the last General ....

Felix Hughes of Capt Thomas Cantons Company ... ten Shillings ... the last General ....

Joseph Dunn of Capt Thomas Cantons Company ... ten Shillings ... the last General ....

Frederick Unsult of Captain Thomas Catons Company ... ten Shillings ... the last General ....

Jacob Brown of Captain Thomas Catons Company ... ten Shillings ... the last General ....

James Morgan of Captain Thomas Catons Company ... ten Shillings ... the last General ....

John Morgan of Captain Thomas Catons Company ... ten Shillings ... the last General ....

Matthias Swin of Captain Thomas Catons Company ... ten Shillings ... the last General ....

John Swin of Captain Thomas Catons Company ... ten Shillings ... the last General ....

Matthias Swin Junnr of Capt Thomas Catons Company ... ten Shillings ... the last General ....

Robert Caton of Captain Thomas Catons Company ... ten Shillings ... the last General ....

Wm Jackson of Captain Thomas Catons Company ... ten Shillings ... the last General ....

[page 48] John Stewart of Captain Thomas Catons Company ... ten Shillings ... the last General ....

William Smith (of **Cap⁴ Thomas Catons** Company on the Motion of the said Captain) be discharged of further duty at Musters

John McCoy of **Captain Thomas Catons** Company ... ten Shillings ... the last General ....

David Shaine of **Cap⁴ Thomas Cantons** Company ... ten Shillings ... the last General ....

Richard Smith of **Cap⁴ Thomas Catons** Company ... ten Shillings ... the last General ....

Job Harrington of **Cap⁴ Thomas Catons** Company ... ten Shillings ... the last General ....

Thomas Copely of **Cap⁴ Thomas Catons** Company ... ten Shillings ... the last Generalmuster

On the Motion of **Robert Morgan**

Ordered that the Treasurer repay him ten Shillings a fine Inflicted on him at the last Court Martial

William Kilp of **Cap⁴ John Funks** Company ... forty Shillings ... three private & one General ....

Cristian Luther of **Cap⁴ John Funks** Company ... forty Shillings ... three private & one General ....

[page 48-A] **Adam Kilp** of **Captain John Funks** Company ... forty Shillings ... three private & one General ....

Benjamin Lamey of **Captain John Funks** Company ... forty shillings ... three private & one general ....

Jacob Stover of **Captain John Funks** Compamy ... forty shillings ... three private & one general ....

John Funkhouser Jun of **Cap⁴ John Funks** Company ... ten Shillings ... the last General muster

John Funk Junʳ of **Captain John Funks** Company ... thirty shillings ... two private & one general ....

Christian Crabell of **Captain John Funks** Company ... twenty shillings ... one private & one general ....

John Martin of **Captain John Funks** Company ... forty shillings ... three private & one general ....

Jacob Bowman son of **Christian Bowman** of **Cap⁴ John Funks** Company ... ten Shillings ... the last General muster

Christian Walter of **Captain John Funks** Company ... ten Shillings ... the last General muster

Christian Hockman of **Captain John Funks** Company ... forty shillings ... three private & one general ....

[page 49] **Peter Hockman** of **Cap⁴ John Funks** Company ... forty shillings ... three private & one general ....

Daniel Obryan of **Cap⁴ Robert Peariss** Company ten Shillings ... the last General muster

Richard Sturman of **Capt Robert Peariss** Company ...three Shillings ... last General muster without a Gun

David Forbes of **Capt Robert Pearis** Company on the motion of the said Captain be discharged of further Duty at Musters

William Cockron (of **Capt John Greenfields** Company on his Motion be discharged of further Duty at Musters

John Collens of **Capt John Greenfields** Company ... ten Shillings ... one private ....

Phillip Bush of **Capt John Greenfields** Company ... twenty shillings ... two private ....

Joshua Baker of **Capt John Greenfields** Company ... ten shillings ... one private ....

Benjamin Grubb of **Capt John Greenfields** Company is fined for appearing at one private & one General ....

[page 49-A] **George Martin** of **Captain John Greenfields** Company ... ten shillings ... one private ....

Thomas Wood of **Captain John Greenfields** Company ... twenty shillings ... two private ....

Daniel Bush of **Captain John Greenfields** Company ... ten shillings ... one private ....

Jacob Castleman of **Captain John Greenfields** Company ... ten shillings ... one private ....

Peter Foreman of **Captain John Greenfields** Company ... twenty shillings ... two private ....

John Quirk of **Captain John Greenfields** Company ... ten shillings ... one private ....

David Reece of **Captain John Greenfields** Company ... ten shillings ... one private ....

John McKemme of **Capt John Greenfields** Company ... ten shillings ... one private ....

[page 50] **Andrew Fridley** of **Capt John Greenfields** Company ... ten shillings ... one private ....

John Hooper of **Capt John Greenfields** Company ... ten shillings ... one private ....

Christopher Aldrid of **Capt John Greenfields** Company ... ten shillings ... one private ....

Michael Aldred of **Capt John Greenfields** Company ... ten shillings ... one private ....

John Skelding of **Capt John Greenfields** Company ... ten shillings ... one private ....

Robert Cragan of **Capt John Greenfields** Company ... ten shillings ... one private ....

William Laughery of **Capt John Greenfields** Company ... ten shill^gs ... one private ....

Patrick Cunningham of **Capt John Greenfields** Company ... ten shillings ... one private ....

[page 50-A] **Samuel Maryfield** of **Capt John Greenfields** Company ... ten shillings ... one private ....

John Humphrys of **Capt John Greenfields** Company ... ten shillings ... one private ....

John Nash (of **Capt John Greenfields** Company on his Motion) be discharged of further Duty at Musters

David Primpain of **Capt John Greenfields** Company ... ten shillings ... one private ....

Phillip Babb (of **Capt John Greenfields** Company on his Motion be discharged of further duty at Musters

Godfry Humbart of **Captain John Greenfields** Company ... ten shillings ... one private ....

Leonard Extine of **Captain John Greenfields** Company ... ten shillings ... one private ....

Jacob Miller of **Capt John Dentons** Company ... forty shillings ... three private & one general ....

Abraham Miller of **Ca^pt John Dentons** Company ... forty shillings ... three private & one general ....

[page 51] **Christopher Crabell** of **Ca^pt John Dentons** Company ... thirty shillings ... two private & one general ....

Conrad Brinker of **Ca^pt John Dentons** Company ... ten shillings ... one private ....

Ulrick Rora of **Captain John Dentons** Company ... forty shillings ... three private & one general ....

Francis Weighgle of **Ca^pt John Dentons** Company ... forty shillings ... three private & one general ....

David Clem of **Captain John Dentons** Company ... ten shillings ... one private ....

Cristian Stickly of **Ca^pt John Dentons** Company ... thirty shillings ... two private & one general ....

Patrick MKenny of **Ca^pt John Dentons** Company ... thirty shillings ... two private & one general ....

Then the Court Adjourned till the next Day ten Eight Oclock

John Hite

[page 51-A] At a court Martial Held for Frederick County on Satterday the 10th Day of October 1761

Present

John Hite Esqr Col°
Lewis Stephens Esqr Maj^r
Joseph McDowell
John Allen
John Funk
John Greenfield
Thomas Speak
Lewis Moore   Gent Captains
Cornelias Ruddle
Marques Calmese
John Schene
Robert Pearis
William Crawford

On the Motion of **George Bethell**
the Treasurer repay him the same sum which he was fined at the last Court Martial
Vinsent Hubbs of **Capt Lewis Moores** Company ... ten shillings ... one general ....
Jacob Harlon of **Capt Lewis Moores** Company ... ten shillings ... the last general muster
Randolph Kennerly of **Capt Lewis Moores** Company ... ten shillings ... the last general muster
Alexander McAdams of **Capt Lewis Moores** Company ... ten shillings ... the last general muster
[page 52] **Robert Eaton** of **Capt Lewis Moores** Company ... ten shillings ... the last general muster
James Morriss of **Capt Thomas Speaks** Company ... twenty shillings ... one private & one general ....
Charles Lowery of **Capt Thomas Speaks** Company ... ten shillings ... one private ....
John Walton Junr of **Capt Thomas Speaks** Company ... ten shillings ... one private ....
William Johnston of **Capt Thomas Speaks** Company ... ten shillings ... one private ....
William Cook of **Capt Thomas Spikes** Company ... twenty shillings ... two private ....
Michael Craven of **Capt Thomas Spiks** Company ... thirty shillings ... three private ....

John Logan of Ca^pt^ Thomas Speaks Company ... ten shillings ... one private ....

Isaac Lindsay of Capt Thos Speaks Company ... ten shillings ... one private ....

[page 52-A] **Timothy Bean** of Ca^p^t Thomas Speaks Company ... ten shillings ... one private ....

Richd Egleon of Captain Thomas Speaks Company ... ten shillings ... one private ....

Michael Davis of Captain Thomas Speaks County [sic] ... ten shillings ... one private ....

Andrew Norwood of Ca^pt^ Thomas Speaks Company ... thirty shillings ... two private & one general ....

Thomas Lindsay Junr of Ca^pt^ Thomas Speaks Company ... ten shillings ... one private ....

Richard Horsly of Ca^p^t Thomas Speaks Company ... ten shillings ... one private ....

Abraham Lindsay of Ca^pt^ Thomas Speaks Company ... ten shillings ... one private ....

William Masterson of Ca^pt^ Thomas Speaks Company ... ten shillings ... one private ....

John Lindsay Jun of Ca^p^t Thomas Speaks Company ... Three Shillings for appearing at muster without a Gun

[page 53] **John Reagan Junr** of Ca^pt^ Thomas Speaks Company is fined Three Shillings for appearing at muster without a gun

James Fowler Junr of Ca^pt^ Thomas Speaks Company is fined Three Shillings for appearing at muster without a gun

Moses Nolton of Captain Thomas Speakes Company is fined three shillings for appearing at without a gun.

John Sim of Capt Joseph M^c^Dowells Company on the motion of the s^d^ Capt be discharged of further Duty at musters

Moses Stricker of Capt John Allens Company on the motion of the s^d^ Captain discharged of further duty at musters

John Nicholas of Capt Marques Calmese Company is fined Three Shillings for apppearing at muster without a firelock

Peter Woolf of Capt Marques Calmes's Company is on the motion of the s^d^ Captain discharged of further duty at Musters

Joseph Burden of Capt Marques Calmese Company ... twenty shillings ... one private & one general ....

Nathaniel Curry of Capt Marques Calmes Company ... thirty shillings ... two private & one general ....

[page 53-A] **Alexander Oglivy** of Capt Marques Calmese Company ... fifty shillings ... four private & one general ....

Samuel Wilcocks of **Capt Marques Calmeses** Company Thirteen shillings ... one private muster & appearing at the General muster without a firelock

James Crane of **Capt Marques Calmese** Company ... thirty shillings ... two private & one general ....

Francis Prince of **Capt Marques Calmese** Company ... twenty shillings ... one private & one general ....

George Arnold (of **Capt Marques Calmes** Company on his motion) be discharged of further duty at musters

John Painter (of **Capt Marques Calmes** Company on the Motion of **Robert Rutherford**) be discharged of further duty at musters

John Painter Junr of **Captain Marques Calmese** Company ... fifty shillings ... four private & one General ....

Robert Painter of **Capt Marques Calmee** Company ... fifty shillings ... four private & one general ....

[page 54] **Samuel Humber** of **Capt Marques Calmes** Company ... fifty shillings ... four private & one general ....

Robert Hains of **Captain Marques Calmes** Company ... fifty shillings ... four private & one general ....

William Berry of **Capt Marques Calmes** Company ... fifty shillings ... four private & one general ....

Thomas Branson of **Capt Marques Calmes** Company ... fifty shillings ... four private & one general ....

Jacob Moore of **Captain Cornelias Ruddles** Company ... Five pounds for accepting of a Leuitenants Commission in the s^d Company & Refusing to swear into the same

Reubin Moore of **Captain Cornelias Ruddles** Company ... ten shillings ... the last general muster

Jackson Allen of **Captain Cornelias Ruddle** Company ... forty shillings ... three private & one general ....

Joseph Allen of **Captain Cornelias Ruddle** Company ... forty shillings ... three private & one general ....

William Moore of **Captain Cornelias Ruddle** Company ... ten shillings ... the last Genl muster

William White Junr of **Capt Cornelias Ruddle** Company ... ten shillings ... the last General Muster

[page 54-A] **William Clarke** of **Capt Cornelias Ruddles** Company ... ten shillings ... the last general muster

John Neffe of **Capt Cornelias Ruddles** Company ... forty shillings ... three private & one general ....

John Clarke of **Capt Cornelias Ruddles** Company ... ten shillings ... the last General muster

Francis Neffe of **Captain Cornelias Ruddles** Company ... forty shillings ... three private & one general ....

Abraham Neffe of **Captain Cornelias Ruddles** Company ... forty shillings ... three private & one general ....

John Seveer of **Cap⁺ Cornelias Ruddles** Company ... ten shillings ... the last General muster

Nicholas Schorn Junʳ of **Captain Cornelias Ruddles** Company ... ten shillings ... the last General muster

Edward Painter of **Cap⁺ Cornelias Ruddles** Company ... ten shillings ... the last General Muster

Thomas Painter of **Cap⁺ Cornelias Ruddles** Company ... ten shillings ... the last general muster

Henry Brown of **Cap⁺ Cornelias Ruddles** Company ... ... ten shillings ... the last General muster

[page 55] **John Beason** of **Cap⁺ Cornelias Ruddles** Company ... ten shillings ... one general ....

Timothy Aroack Junʳ of **Cap⁺ Cornelias Ruddles** Company ... ten shillings ... the last general muster

Joseph Hill of **Captain Cornelias Ruddles** Company ... ten shillings ... the last General muster

John Hill of **Captain Cornelias Ruddles** Company ... ten shillings ... the last General Muster

Robert Calldwell of **Cap⁺ Cornelias Ruddles** Company ... ten shillings ... the last General Muster

Westly White of **Captain Cornelias Ruddles** Company ... ten shillings ... the last General muster

Daniel Nowland Junʳ of **Cap⁺ Cornelias Ruddles** Company ... ten shillings ... the last General Muster

Abraham Drist of **Cap⁺ Cornelias Ruddles** Company ... ten shillings ... the last General Muster

Balser Peters of **Captain Cornelias Ruddles** Company ... ten shillings ... the last General muster

Andrew Nelson of **Cap⁺ Cornelias Ruddles** Company ... ten Shillings ... the last General muster

Adam Reynard of **Cap⁺ Cornelias Ruddles** Company ... ten shillings ... the last General muster

[page 55-A] **Phillip Harpine** of **Captain Cornelias Ruddles** Company ... ten shillings ... the last General muster

Charles Stapleton of **Captain Cornelias Ruddles** Company ... ten shillings ... the last General muster

Jacob Hammer of **Cap⁺ Cornelias Ruddles** Company ... ten shillings ... the last General Muster

Symon Horn of **Captain Cornelias Ruddles** Company ... ten shillings ... the last General Muster

George Shade (of **Capt John Greenfields** Company on his Motion) be repaid the same Sum that he was fined at the last Court Martial ....

Daniel Mitheny of **Capt William Crawfords** Company ... ten shillings ... the last General Muster

John Wilson of **Capt William Crawfords** Company ... twenty shillings ... one private & one General ....

William Coil of **Capt William Crawfords** Company ... ten shillings ... the last General Muster

George Davis of **Capt William Crawfords** Company ... ten shillings ... the last General Muster

James Shirly of **Capt William Crawfords** Company ... ten shillings ... the last General muster

James McCoy of **Capt Henry Spears** Company ... ten shillings ... the last General Muster

[page 56] On the motion of **Lt Abraham Keller**

John Davis Of **Captain Henry Spears** Company be discharged of further Duty at Musters

Henry Harden Junr of **Capt Henry Spears** Company ... ten shillings ... the last General Muster

On the Motion of **Lt Abraham Keller**

Walter Cunningham of **Capt Henry Spears** Company be discharged of further Duty at Musters

Moses McCoy of **Capt Henry Spears** Company ... twenty shillings ... one private & one general ....

Zachariah McCoy of **Capt Henry Spears** Company ... twenty shillings ... one private & one Genl ....

Enock Job of **Captain Henry Spears** Company ... ten shillings ... the last General Muster

William Davis of **Capt Henry Spears** Company ... ten shillings ... one general ....

Zackariah Campbell of **Capt Henry Spears** Company ... ten shillings ... the last General Muster

Elisha Riggins of **Capt Henry Spears** Company ... twenty shillings ... one private & one general ....

[page 56-A] **John Cunningham** of **Capt Henry Spears** Company ... ten shillings ... the last General Muster

John Combs of **Captain Henry Spears** Company ... ten shillings ... the last General Muster

Henry Hardin Sen (of **Capt Henry Spears** Company on the motion of **Lt Abraham Keller**) be discharged of further duty at musters

Bazell Daniel of Capt **Henry Spears** Company ... ten shillings ... the last General Muster

John Odell of **Captain Henry Spears** Company ... ten shillings ... the last General Muster

Captain John Schene ... ten pounds for not appearing with his Company at the last General muster nor making any Return of the Same

On the motion of **Captain John Schene**

Ordered that the Treasurer repay him the same sum which he was fined at the last Court Martial

On the motion of **Capt John Schene**

Ordered that **John Rodes** of his Company be discharged of further duty at Musters

On the motion of **Capt John Schean**

Ordered that **Daniel Stover** of his Company be discharged of further duty at Musters

On the motion of **Capt John Schene**

Ordered that **Phillip Crame** of his Company be discharged of further duty at Musters

On the motion of **Capt Lewis Moore**

Ordered that **Nathaniel Bell** of his Company be discharged of further duty at Musters

[page 57] Ordered that the Sheriff pay **Robert Rutherford** Fifteen pounds Curr^t Money as his Sallery for his Services at this present Court Martial ....

Ordered that the Sheriff have fifty Shillings for his Attendance at this Court Martial ....

Ordered that the Clark diliver the several orders of this Court Martial to the Sheriff

Ordered that the Sheriff Recieve the Several orders of this Court Martial from the Clark & Collect the same according to law & account for the same with **Capt John Greenfield** treasurer

Ordered that **Captain John Greenfield** be continued Treasurer ....

Then the Court adjourned till the next Court Martial

                                                                    John Hite

[END]

INDEX

Brook
  Thomas 28
Brooks
  David 21
Brown
  Henry 52
  Jacob 45
  Richard 26
  William 25
Brumfield
  Thomas 32
Bryan
  John 29
Bryn
  James 7
Buck
  Charles 27
  Thomas 27
Bufton
  Isaac 7
Burden
  Joseph 50
Burge
  Henry 12
Burkham
  Solomon 26
Burner
  Archart 16
Burrage
  Thomas 35
Burrows
  William 29
Bush
  Daniel 38, 47
  Macksamelaon 37
  Maxsamillion 14
  Phillip 29, 38, 41,
    47
Byrns
  William 20, 34
Caity
  Michael 6
Calemese / Calemus
    /Calimese
  Captain 35
  Marquis 18, 19, 20,
    31, 33, 35, 41-44,
    49-51

William 39
Calldwell
  Robert 52
Callimes / Callimese
    (see Calemese)
Calmee / Calmemus
    (see Calemese)
Calmes / Calmese (see
    Calemese)
Calmon
  Matthias 28
Calvil
  James 3
Cambel / Cambell
  Joseph 15
  Thomas 7
Campbell
  Duggel 33
  John 38
  Zackariah 53
Canton
  Thomas 44-46
Carder
  Edward 33
Carson
  Simon 3
Carter
  Richard 22
Castleman
  Jacob 47
Castles
  James 25
Caton
  Robert 45
  Thomas 18, 35, 41,
    42, 44-46
Cator
  James 9
Cave
  Joseph 14
Chambers
  William 44
Chapman
  Edward 39
Cherry
  John 45
  William 44
Chester

Thomas 27
Chinnoath
  John 44
  William 44
Christman
  Jacob 6
Clark / Clarke
  James 28, 33
  John 51
  William 51
Clem
  David 48
Closime
  John 11
Cloud
  Henry 10
Cockley
  Jacob 34
Cockron
  William 47
Cocks (see also Cox)
  William 9, 10
Coffield
  George 11
  Valentine 12
Coffman
  Augustine 11
Coil
  William 53
Collens
  Edmond 37
  John 47
Collins
  Edward 24
  Francis 30
  James 37
  Thomas 19
Colman
  Matthias 38
Colvil
  Joseph 6
Combs
  John 53
  Joseph 7, 19
Comer
  Michael 15
Conrod
  Frederick 28

Cook
  William 40, 49
Cooper
  Joseph 27
  Thomas 26
Copely
  Thomas 46
Corker
  George 42
Cotzman
  David 15
Countz
  Henry 13
  John 15
  Nicholas 13
Cox (see also Cocks)
  Freind 25
Crabbtree
  James 21
Crabell
  Christian 46
  Christopher 48
Cragan
  Robert 47
Craine
  James 22
Crame
  Phillip 54
Crane
  James 51
Craven
  Michael 49
Cravens
  Michael 40
Crawford
  William 43, 49, 53
Crissman
  Abraham 23
Crumbley
  John 31
Crume
  John 14
Cuningham
  Adam 23
  Edward 24
  Walter 23
Cunningham
  Adam 36

John 53
Patrick 48
Walter 36, 53
Curlet
  William 23
Curry
  Nathaniel 19, 39, 50
Curtis
  Daniel 14
Daniel
  Bazell 54
  John 24
  William 24, 37
Daring
  Everhart 29
Daugherty
  Nathaniel 9
Daves
  William 8
Davis
  George 53
  John 9, 33, 53
  Michael 50
  Thomas 10
  William 53
Denny
  Handell 29
Denton
  John 11, 28, 31, 33,
    35, 36, 41, 48
Dillingar
  Frederick 13
Dillon
  Luke 32
  William 44
Dinton
  John 3
Dobbin
  William 44
Dooly
  Patrick 32
Doran
  Thomas 30
Dorster
  James 31
  Thomas 33
  William 31
Dotson

John 12
Drist
  Abraham 52
Duckworth
  John 3
Dunbar / Dunbarr
  James 9, 31
Dunn
  Joseph 45
Dyer
  John 26
Ealy
  Isaec 25
Eaton
  Robert 49
Edwards
  Peter 10
  Robert 14
Egleon
  Richard 50
Eldridge
  Thomas 7
Emry
  George 25
Enoch
  Henry 21
Evans
  John 20, 33
  William 34
Ewing
  William 22
Extine
  Leonard 48
Fairfax 24
  George William 3,
    17
  Lord 3, 17, 18, 24,
    30
Farrar
  George 42
Fauccet
  Richard 23
Faw
  Pauleer 29
Feigh Helm (see
  Helm)

Fight
  Tehobald 4
  Theobald 28
Fisher
  Frederick 12
Fleming
  John 43
Fletcher
  Thomas 32
Foccet
  John 23
Folio
  Richard 43
Folles
  Isaac 33
Fon Feigh Helm
  see Helm 34
Forbes
  David 47
Foreman
  Peter 47
Forster
  William 36
Fouccet
  John 23
  Richard 23
Fowler
  James 50
Fox
  Adam 13
  Hugh 10
Fravel
  Henry 4
Frederick
  Bostion 15
  / Fridley
Fridley
  Andrew 38, 47
Funk
  Jacob 3, 10, 11
  John 4, 18, 24, 28,
    33, 35, 41-44, 46,
    49
  John, Jr. 17, 46
  Peter 11
Funkhouser
  John, Jr. 46
Gabbert

Gotlip 4
Gann
  John 27
  Samuel 3
George
  Joseph 7
  Thomas 20
Gilham
  William 29
Gill
  Thomas 10
Gimblet
  Jacob 17
Glass
  Phillip 42
  Samuel 23
Goldsberry
  Thomas 25, 43
Goodbread
  Phillip 13
Goodlet
  Robert 19
Gor
  Mark 13
Gotlip
  John 16
Gray
  Robert 4
Green
  Regnal 5
  Thomas 5
Greenfield (see also
    Griendfield)
  John 41-42, 47-49,
    53, 54
Griendfield /
    Grienfield (see
    also Greenfield)
  John 31, 36-38, 40
Grisby
  Benjamin 15
Grubb
  Benjamin 47
  Philip 15
Grubbs
  Benjah 35
Grymes
  Edward 10

Hackney
  Aaron 31
Hagan
  Barnaby 43
Hagen
  James 30
Hails
  John 6
Hains
  Abraham 8
  Robert 19, 35, 51
Hainy
  John 28
Halfpenny
  Robert 28
Halterman
  John 15
Hammer
  Jacob 52
Hammet
  Robert 14
Hammon
  Absalam 9
Hammons
  Obadiah 14
Hampton
  George 9
  Henry 19
  Joseph 9
Handshaw
  John 31
Hankins
  John 36, 37
Hanks
  John 4
Hannon
  Jacob 10
Harden / Hardin
  Henry 23, 36
  Henry, Jr. 53
  Henry, Sr. 53
  John 3, 8, 9, 17-18,
    24-26
Hardwick
  Hasle 20
Harisson
  Samuel 21

Harker
  Phillip 3
Harlon
  Jacob 49
Harmond
  Richard 37
Harper
  Robert 26
Harpine
  Phillip 52
Harrington
  Job 46
Harris
  Christian 15
  John 23
Harrisson
  Benjamin 39
Harrol
  Moses 10
  Richard 10
Harry
  William 4
Hart
  Thomas 5
Hartly
  John 43
Hasewell
  Samuel 27
Haymaker
  Adam 38, 42
Hedge
  Jonas 20
  Joshua 20
Helfenstone
  Peter 28
  Phillip 30
Helm
  John Frederick Fon
    Feigh 34
  Meredith 3
Henry
  George 8
  James 43
Heskell
  Christopher 42
Heywood
  John 5
  Moses 5

Hiatt
  George 25
  Simeon 25
Hicks
  William 6, 21
Highly
  George 21
Hill
  John 52
  Joseph 52
  Thomas 39
Hite
  John 18, 24, 31, 36,
    40, 41, 48, 49, 54
Hockman
  Christian 46
  Peter 46
Hodgson
  Robert 33
Hodson
  Robert 6
Hoffman
  George 13
Hoge
  George 22
  James 38
Hogg
  James 43
Holingsworth
  George 7
Holliday
  Samuel 27
Hollingbaugh
  John George 21
Holmes
  Richard 8
Hoof
  Laurance 42
Hooper
  John 47
Hopkins
  Humphrey 8
Horn
  Symon 53
Horner
  Joseph 28
Horsly
  Richard 50

Hotzenbeller
  Stephen 34
Hough
  Lawrence 28
  Lewis 29
House
  John 3
Howart
  James 4
Howell
  Francis 20
  Thomas 7, 35
Hubbs
  Joseph 7
  Vincent 49
Huddle
  Charles 43
Huff
  Laurance 38
Hughes
  Felix 45
  Ralph 14
  William 24
Hultz
  John 9
  Josiah 44
Humbar
  Samuel 35
Humbart
  Godfry 48
Humber
  Samuel 19, 51
Humble
  Michael 42
Hume
  David 37
  Thomas 37
Humphreys
  John 48
Humphrys
  John 9, 25
Hurt
  John 37
Husk
  William 26
Hustand
  Henry 15

Huston
　James 35
Hyzer
　Charles 16
Iler
　Mark 44
Ilor
　Mark 13
Ireson
　James 36
Issaccs
　Elisha 22
Jack
　James 45
Jackson
　Robert 30
　William 14, 45
Jameson
　George 35
Jamison
　George 19
Jinnins
　Edward 7
Job
　Enock 53
　John 7
　Joshua 24, 37
Johnson
　Richard 8
Johnston
　Jacob 45
　Richard 39
　William 49
Johnstone
　William 39
Jolliff
　Edmond 32
　James 6
　William 5
　William, Jr. 32
Jones
　Morgan 13
Kelleh
　Daniel 39
Keller
　Abraham 43, 53
Kelly
　Benjamin 8

Kennerly
　Randolph 49
Keys
　Humphrey 8
Killer
　Abraham 43, 44
　Abram 43
Kilp
　Adam 46
　William 46
Kinah
　Ulrick 13
King
　James 10, 20
Kiplinger
　Daniel 16
　Philip 16
Lacy
　John 37, 43
Lahugh
　John 27
　Spencer 27
Lamey
　Benjamin 46
Larack
　John 34
Laughery
　William 48
Leadsome
　Thomas 29
Leaman
　Jonah 21
Lemen
　Alexander 36
　Robert 36
　Thomas 37
Lender
　George 20
Libas
　Wiliam 26
Limeburger
　John 14
Lindsay
　Abraham 50
　Isaac 50
　John, Jr. 50
　Thomas, Jr. 50
Lindsey

David 19
　Edmund, Jr. 9
　Isaac 22
　John 18
Linsey
　John 3, 5
Little
　George 11
　John 10
Lockard
　William 21
Lodwith
　William 44
Logan
　James 45
　John 40, 50
Lommonah
　Jacob 14
Long
　Paul 18
Lossly
　Thomas 29
Love
　Thomas 39
Low
　Abraham 32
　John 16
Lowery / Lowry
　Charles 39, 49
Loyd
　James 5
　John 10
Luther
　Cristian 46
Maden
　Andrew 13
Maggard
　Christian 15
　David 15
Makall
　Benjamin 8
Marpool
　John 5
Marryfield (see also
　　Maryfield)
　Samuel 23
Marshall
　Daniel 5

Martin
  George 47
  John 46
  Thomas 31, 44
  Thomas Bryan 3,
    17, 18, 24
Marty
  John 4
Maryfield (see also
    Marryfield)
  Samuel 48
Mason
  Samuel 40
Masterson
  John 39
  William 50
McAdams
  Alexander 49
McCaib
  Patrick 13
McCarty
  Darby 43
  Joseph 8
McCay
  Moses 14
  Zachariah 14
McClon
  Thomas 29
McConnell
  Nathaniel 39
McCoy
  Andrew 27
  James 4, 23, 36, 53
  John 46
  Moses 23, 36, 53
  Robert 26
  Zachariah 23, 36,
    53
McCuing
  Isaac 42
McDaniel
  Patrick 9
McDowell
  Joseph 31, 34,
    41-43, 49, 50
McGudgion
  John 7
McKemme

John 47
McKenny (see also
    MKenny)
  George 44
  James 11
McNeal
  James 41
McNiel
  James 37
McQuin
  Duggell 9
Meisemore
  Peter 29
Mercer
  James 40
  John 44
MercerSmith
  Henry 33
Messersmith
  Henry 29
Milbourn
  Robert 29
Miller
  Abraham 13, 20,
    36, 48
  Jacob 13, 35, 48
  John 4, 11
  William 26, 27, 34
Minor
  Burger 10
Mire
  John 11
  Michael 16
Mires
  John 6
Mitheny
  Daniel 53
MKenny (see also
    McKenny)
  Patrick 48
Moon
  Jacob 31
Moore
  Anthony 28
  Isaac 33
  Jacob 10, 51
  Lewis 31-33, 36, 41,
    44, 49, 54

Reubin 51
  William 51
Morgan
  Edward 21
  Ezekial 27
  Isaac 42
  James 27, 45
  John 3, 45
  Mordicai 21
  Robert 22, 39, 44,
    46
Morgin
  Richard 3, 5, 18
Morley
  Richard 17
Morriss
  James 49
Mounts
  John 9
Murphey
  Darbey 8
  James 26
Nash
  John 48
Neffe
  Abraham 52
  Francis 52
  John 51
Neil
  Widow 25
  William 25
Nelson
  Andrew 52
Netherton
  Henry 44
Newcome
  Daniel 26
Nicholas
  John 50
  Richard 12
Niecwanger
  John 34
Niel
  Francis 39
Nizely
  Samuel 13
Noble
  William 45

Nodle
  Jacob 12
Nolton
  Moses 50
North
  John 23
Norwood
  Andrew 50
Nowland
  Daniel, Jr. 52
  Stephen 4
Obryan
  Daniel 46
ODell
  John 24, 54
  Nehimiah 4
  Samuel 3, 13, 14,
    17, 18
Oglevey
  Alexander 35
Oglivy
  Alexander 50
Oler
  Adam 42
Oliver
  John 27
Otto
  Tobias 30
Overhall
  William 43
Owerson
  Siman 6
Pack
  George 45
  Samuel 45
  Thomas 45
Padgett
  Reubin 37
Pain
  Adam 44
Painter
  Edward 52
  John 12, 35, 51
  John, Jr. 51
  John, Sr. 19
  Peter 16
  Robert 19, 35, 51
  Thomas 52

Paris
  Robert 24
Parken (see also
    Parkin)
  Isaac 7
Parker
  Nicholas 36, 41
Parkin (see also
    Parken)
  Isaac 6, 17, 18
  Issaac 3
Parkins
  Isaac 28-31, 33, 34,
    36, 38
  Vollentine 22
Parris
  Robert 22
Paul
  Robert 20
Pearis / Peariss
  Robert 18, 38-39,
    41, 43, 44, 46,
    47, 49
Pearpoint
  Larkin 24, 37
Pearriss (see also
    Pearis)
  Robert 39
Pearson
  Benjamin 8
  Samuel 8
Pearsons
  Samuel 25
Perchman
  Nicholas 22
Percles
  John 40
Perkins
  Isaac 18
  Isace 24
Perry
  Peter 30
  Thomas 26
Perrygoy
  Henry 34
Peters
  Balser 52
  Henry 12

John 22, 28
Paul 28
Peulson
  Peter 9
Phillips
  Jonathan 25
  William 30
Picket
  Richard 22
Pierce
  George 27
  John 38
Pippin
  John Henry 16
Pontz
  Jacob 16
Poore
  Samuel 39
Porough
  Michael 15
Posegate
  Thomas 8
Postgate
  Thomas 44
Powell
  Caleb 27
Pressor
  Henry 16
Price
  Benjamin 26
  Edward 14
  William 9
Priest
  William 11
Primpain
  David 48
Prince
  Francis 51
Pritchard
  Daniel 4
Proston
  Martin 28
Pugh
  Azariah 5
  Thomas 4
Quirk
  John 47

Ragon
  Charles 23
Rankins
  William 8
Rantz
  Frederick 34
Reagan
  John, Jr. 50
Redmon
  Jeremiah 39
Reece
  David 47
  Morriss, Jr. 5
  Morriss, Sr. 5
  William 32
Reed
  Edward 43
  John 6
Reynard
  Adam 52
Rheymick
  Phillip 25
Rich
  Conrood 15
Ridgway
  John 5
  Josiah 32
  Richard 32
Riggins
  Elisha 53
RillGore
  Robert 22
Rinker
  Henry 34
Rinuller
  Nicholas 34
Rionuller
  Nicholas 34
Roberts
  William 9, 22, 39
Roden
  William 27
Rodes
  John 54
Rodgers
  Edward 3, 8, 18, 35, 42
  Edward, Sr. 19

William 13
Rodinhaver
  David 11
Rogers
  Captain 8
  Edward 5, 44
Roller
  Martin 12
Rora
  Ulrick 48
Ross
  Alexander 33, 41
Rought
  George 19
Rout
  John 35
  Peter 19
Rowlings
  Stephen 44
Rubel
  George 4
Ruble
  Peter 32
  Samuel 32
Rucry
  Richard 5
Ruddell / Ruddle
  Archabald 28, 33
  Captain 34
  Cornelius 3, 10, 17, 31, 44, 49, 51-53
Russel / Russell
  Stephen 21
  William 34
Rust
  George 4
Rutherford
  Robert 3, 18, 40, 44, 51, 54
Sample
  William 7
Sanders
  Benjamin 42
Satterfield
  Benjamin 9
Satturfield
  Benjamin 26
Saverrel

Leonard 5
Schean
  John 54
Schene / Schene (see also Skene)
  John 34, 41, 49, 54
Schorn
  Nicholas, Jr. 52
Scot
  John 9
Seabourn
  George 20
Self
  Philip 11
Sell
  George 30
Seller
  Adam 11
  George 4
Selser
  Lewis 27
Seveer
  John 52
  William 43
Sevier
  William 37
Shade
  George 29, 38, 53
Shaine
  David 46
  William 30
Shanes
  David 6
Sharp
  Thomas, Jr. 23
Shaver
  Jacob 16
Shirley
  Robert 24
Shirly
  James 53
Shmearer
  John 28
Shober
  Frederick 16
Shoemaker
  Henry 30

Shoeman
  Stephen 12
Shovelberger
  Jacob 26
Shrock
  Nicholas 38, 41
Sim
  John 50
Simpson
  John 31
Sisk
  James 37
Skelding
  John 47
Skene (see also
    Schene)
  John 34
Skidmore
  Joseph 25
Small
  John 21
Smallsoffer
  Christopher 4
Smith
  Benjamin 27, 39
  Jeremiah 3-5, 18
  John 16
  Richard 46
  Thomas 38
  William 46
Snap / Snapp
  John 22
  John, Sr. 6
Sneed
  George 25
Snell
  William 6, 19
Snickers
  Edward 22
Speak / Speake (see
    also Speke)
  Henry 36
  Thomas 18, 21, 22,
    24, 41, 49
Speakes / Speaks
  Thomas 42, 44, 49,
    50
Spear (see also Spere)

Henry 23, 24, 31,
  36, 37, 53
Spears
  Henry 18, 41, 43,
    44, 53, 54
Speke (see also
    Speak)
  Henry 37
  Thomas 31, 36, 39,
    40
Spere (see also Spear)
  Henry 37
Spiker
  Julias 29
Spikes
  Thomas 49
Spiks
  Thomas 49
Stapleton
  Charles 52
Stedman
  James 26
Stephen
  Lewis 3, 5, 6, 31
Stephens
  Henry 22, 33
  Lewis 22, 23, 26,
    33, 36, 41, 49
Stewart
  John 28, 45
Sticklor
  John 23
Stickly
  Cristian 48
Stokes
  Isaac 7, 20
Stoney Creek 12
Stonis
  Lewis 16
Stover
  Daniel 14, 24, 37,
    54
  Jacob 46
  Samuel 37
Stricker
  Moses 50
Strickler
  Jacob 16

Joseph 16
Stuart
  John 38
  Robert 7
Stultz
  Anthony 13
Sturman
  Richard 47
Summer
  Henry 28
Summers
  Joseph 15
Sutherland
  Daniel 34
Swaringin
  Thomas 17
Swearingin
  Thomas 18, 24
Sweringin
  Thomas 20, 21, 31,
    33, 36, 41
  Van 31, 34, 36, 38,
    41, 42
Swin
  John 45
  Matthias 45
Tann
  John 15
Tanner
  Michael 21
Taviner
  Anthony 29
Taylor
  Charles 13
  Simon 23
  Taylor 14
Temmons
  Edward 22
  John 20
Tharp
  Zebulon 34
Thiltz
  John 9
Thinah
  Ulrick 13
Thomas
  Enos 44
  George 6

Thomas, con't.
  Isaac 25
  Nathaniel 25
Thompson
  Charles 16, 24
  George 29
Thomson
  Joseph 25
Timons
  Samuel 7
Tollifer
  John 14
Tollis
  George 5
Towland
  Patrick 32
Tryat
  Bartholomen 21
Turner
  Anthony 5, 38
Tzitzir
  Jacob 44
Unsult
  Frederick 45
Vagan
  Meoly 30
Vance
  James 42
  Vance 18
  William 3, 17, 24
Vastal
  John 9
Vestall
  John 25
Voltz
  Adam 15
  Mark 11
Von Veigh Helm (see
  Helm)
Walker
  Abel 21
Wallis
  James 14
Walter
  Christian 46
Walton
  John, Jr. 49
Warren

Hugh 26
William 27
Waters
  John 8
Way
  John 26
Weaver
  George 43
Weigell
  Francis 36
Weighgle
  Francis 48
Welton
  Moses 39
White
  Westly 52
  William, Jr. 51
Wilcocks
  Samuel 51
Williams
  James 30
  John 39
  Remembrance 5
  Thomas 39
Williamson
  James 21
Wilson
  James 6
  John 20, 25, 53
Wilt
  Peter 34
Withers
  Ralf 42
Wolf (see Woolf)
Wolfat
  Frederick 11
Wood
  Benjamin 20
  Isaac 14
  Jeremiah 19
  John 7, 15
  Joseph 20
  Thomas 47
  William 14, 20, 35
Woolf
  Peter 50
Worrill
  Charles 9

Wright
  David 6
  George, Jr. 6, 23
  George, Sr. 6, 23
Yates
  William 21
Young
  Samuel 29, 38

www.ingramcontent.com/pod-product-compliance
Lightning Source LLC
Chambersburg PA
CBHW060200070426
42447CB00033B/2243